HUPOMONE
hoop-on-on-ay

*The Journey of a Young Woman Forsaking
Stereotypes & Defying Odds to Become
Who God Called Her to Be*

Amber Underwood

HUPOMONE
hoop-on-on-ay

The Journey of a Young Woman Forsaking
Stereotypes & Defying Odds to Become
Who God Called Her to Be

Amber Underwood

T&J PUBLISHERS

A SMALL INDEPENDENT PUBLISHER WITH A BIG VOICE

Printed in the United States of America by
T&J Publishers (Atlanta, GA.)
www.TandJPublishers.com

@ Copyright 2021 by Amber Underwood

It's always my goal to honor and respect others while using my gifts and talents. Therefore I have changed several names and omitted identifying details in this book not relevant to the message of the book, to protect the privacy of persons that are a part of my story. Like my story, their names and the events that transpired, written and unwritten, are sacred to me. Thank you for understanding and most importantly, thank you for opening your heart to my journey, *Hupomone*.

This book is protected by U.S. and international copyright laws. Reproduction and/or distribution of this book without written permission of the author is prohibited.

Cover Design by Mollie Blackwood of Mollie Joy Designs
Book Format/Layout by Timothy Flemming, Jr.

ISBN: 978-0-578-29137-6

To contact the author, go to:
Email: ambernunderwood3@gmail.com
Facebook: Amber Nicole Underwood
Instagram: @AmberNUnderwood

PRAISES FOR HUPOMONE

"The journey to womanhood is filled with triumphs, challenges, and change. In Hupomone, Amber welcomes us into the distinctive moments that have catalyzed her journey of becoming. I encourage you to carry these pearls of wisdom wherever your journey may lead you; because, the anointing that they were developed from are sure to break any bondage that may hinder you. I am so excited for the rest of the world to experience what I have had the blessed opportunity to watch behind closed doors. This is more than a book. Amber lives this message everyday of her life. You are holding the fruit of her resilience and commitment to keep moving forward no matter the circumstances. I pray that as you read this book, you will not only read of a powerful woman but of the powerful God who created her. His strength, His wisdom, and His purpose living through the pen of a woman who keeps saying "yes" to Him."

—Christian Kelley

"Amber endured, and that's what gives her the right to write. It's her newfound endurance – an endurance from running toward her purpose, come hell or high water, and running through life's storms – that gives this book so much power. As you turn the page, I want to warn you, this book may cause emotional exhaustion. You may be triggered. If you're like me, it was hard to face the hidden parts of myself within the pages of this book because I was still hiding. It wasn't until I read the endurance that follows this page in black and white that I was finally able to experience and live endurance in color. Amber is the good worker Paul writes about. She is unashamed. She correctly explains the Truth because she lived it. She is Hupomone, and I'm overwhelmed that she shared it with me."

—Averie Armstead

"Hupomone is a work of art that I read in its entirety in two days, which is something that I have not done with a book since reading Paulo Coehlo's, The Alchemist. The truth and honesty of her words is impactful and is shared in a way that's relatable. While our exact life experiences are not the same, I saw myself in these words, even in my current season. Trying to Navigate God's plan, while knowing myself and relearning myself at moments where I think I know, is never an easy journey. Stepping out on faith is never what we expect. However, her words show that the journey is worth it, even as we don't know what is next. Choose life, choose God's plans, and the rest will unfold along the way. I feel so inspired for this current season and all that are to come. It has been and is an honor to have watched you on this journey so far and see the fruits manifest this book. Thank you for allowing God to use you and share the truth of yourself with others to inspire greater growth in us all."

—Shannon Walker

"There are no words that can express the blessing I have received by witnessing the process that molded Amber into the woman she has become. I have watched her grow from an infant in her faith to a walking woman, standing strong in her calling. Often times, I believe, when we speak of transformation in our Faith, we tend to think non-believer to believer or a non-churchgoer to a regular church-attendee. However, the blossoming I am talking about in Amber is far different. Her eyes have continued to rest on Him, and, as a result, she has truly developed a type of tunnel vision; no more concern about the optics. More importantly, because she had the courage and obedience to listen to God, she has encouraged me to work on giving up the "me mindset." I have no doubt that those who set their eyes on the words in this book will too be challenged in that same way."

—Karolyn Perry

"Without being aware, Amber and I were handpicked by God, to walk into an outward manifestation of his goodness together. Amber has blazed a trail for me to follow. I believe that God allowed her to proceed me so that I could receive a direct impartation of her mantle and wisdom. I am a witness to her life's journey and her relentless pursuit of fighting to become, even in the midst of struggle. This book is filled with years' of shedding in the presence of God. Each page will grab a piece of you and ultimately encourage you not to shy away from those deep wounded truths. You will be enlightened to the beauty of what seems like an ugly truth, but what God calls a beautiful masterpiece. May this book be a whisper in the wind and a transformational resource to all generations."

—Kayla Hamlett

"You know that feeling when you finish a really good fiction book and wonder what the rest of the story would be? Like now what? I need to know more. That's how I feel about Hupomone. This is a story worth telling. My prayer is that God would use this book in bigger ways than could be imagined. That girl's lives will be changed as they see that they aren't alone in their struggles. The most vulnerable parts of you, written in words and healing others. Thank you Amber for being bold. Thank you for letting others in. What a gift to have read your story and be changed by it."

—Kaylee Tatis

"I met Amber in 2015. She was sitting in a recliner chair across the room, when she began explaining her story to the group. It was a raw and a real version of what she had been through, what she had overcome, and who God was making her to be. I remember being overwhelmed with how vulnerable she was. She had no shame, no fear, only a peace about herself that only God can give. We talked about our faith and where God had brought us, and I knew at that moment that she was a sister for life. As a middle school teacher, I see every day how Hupomone is a necessary part of what every generation needs to walk through this life with boldness and confidence, knowing that God is with you and for you even when you don't feel like He is. Hupomone supersedes feelings and thoughts. It is an unwavering faith, founded on trust and understanding who God was, is, and will always be."

—Madison Gary

"When I think of Amber and her life, as long as I've known her, she embodies the word prolific. She has been fruitful in every capacity of her life and everything has been prolific and excellent. She empowers other people to become the greatest version of themselves, even without her saying a word. She is warm, she is inviting, she is all about community, and she makes sure that every voice is heard. She adapts to the rooms she walks in because the light of God shines on her. Her selfless ventures to foreign places speaks to the high bar she sets to love people you've never met before. As we've ventured out in our friendship, and been through so much, I can say that it is well with her soul. She is ready to hold in spaces that she's never walked in, for she is the woman of the hour and she is ready to claim her title as author. This book will transform your life, your perspective, and the way that you view God. You will find life again and you also will become, as Amber has become.

—Jasmine Morris

"What amazes me about Amber is her unique ability to tell her story in a way that can impact and relate to so many. I realized it's because she listens, follows, and trusts God without doubt. God has a distinct and specific plan for each of us and I am certain that reading this book will urge you to see His plans will always exceed your own, if you let them."

—Tinsley Roberson

"I once read this quote that said 'because I have this crazy idea that my purpose is bigger than me'; the first person I thought of was Amber. Ever since the day I met Amber, she has always challenged me to go deeper in who God has created me to be. I have always told her that her gifts are bigger than her and with the harvesting of this book, I am thankful that God saw fit for me to meet and do life with her. The way God is planning to use her goes far beyond any blog post and any book that she will write. I am honored to speak on the behalf of Amber because I know that every word in this book is from a place of authenticity, obedience, and truth."

—Briah Golder

"A beautiful person, inside and out, Amber is the real deal. She has always generously opened the door to her heart to show you that it is okay to be imperfect. Hupomone is her heart on paper and I can assure you that through her holding nothing back, for you, you will not regret reading this book."

—Tracey Paul

"Steadfast, unwavering, and patient are all words that are synonymous with the word Hupomone. However the thing about words is that they are lifeless if not defined by action.

Within the 10+ years of knowing Amber, there hasn't been a day in which she hasn't lived out the word Hupomone. Fearless, steadfast, and anchored are at her core and all words that she embodies in her everyday life. In her unwavering boldness, through her words in this book, she invites us on a journey of vulnerability, pain, healing, and hope. For the suffering you will find comfort, for the doubting you will find faith, and for the searching, you will find purpose. This is the Hupomone!"

—Jesse Mwakajumba

"A few years ago, my life forever changed when my path crossed paths with Amber's, via a mutual friend. That day Amber became my sister and then my best friend. It's a rarity to have a golden gem as a best friend but God's given me a true treasure. The words she writes can be heavy and light in the same sentence. Similarly to the Word of God; these words don't return void as the Holy Spirit ministers through her writing. Through every written word you'll get a glimpse of a broken and poured out woman as she walks in the wisdom of the Lord."

—Caitlin Wood

"Amber Nicole could hardly know that God would transform her life for His glory. She's spent years seeking nourishment that can only come from time in God's word, prayer, and worship. She's grown in great strides, likely surprising herself at times with how her faith in God and love for him has intensified. Then her cocoon season came. With it, growth looked barer than beautiful, more desperate than delightful, more stretched than safe and in it Amber's past was shredded away. Because God knew transformation was always in the story. He took the remnants of her past and transformed it. In His time, Amber Nicole emerged-mature, beautiful, and surrendered, armed with a story of metamorphosis for the world to see. Grow. Shed. Become."

—Jasmine Prince

"Amber is the epitome of gracefully becoming. She has been sewing into my life since our first encounter – from our friendship, being a confidant, leading our small group, creating inspirational apparel, to now walking out on faith to release Hupomone. Through her evolving journey, she never stopped helping me and others along the way. I am certain Hupomone will speak life into those who partake in it as Amber has personally done for so many. No matter the obstacles she has faced, or adversities that came her way, she allowed life's pressures to develop her faith and strength. As I have seen Amber live out 2 Corinthians 4:8-9, Hupomone is Amber's unselfish vulnerability that has been shared with few now written down to spread light unto many."

—Cynthia D. Green

"Amber's transparency throughout this book is going to show readers that it is okay to have a past. It will prove to readers that although we may stumble throughout our journey with Christ, He will still use us in ways we could never imagine. I am so grateful that Amber is using her story as a platform to help others. I truly believe that this book will inspire and touch every reader who comes in contact with it."

—Ronnae Ravenell

"In the years that I have known Amber, I have witnessed some of her greatest achievements as well as some of the most hurtful experiences of her life. I stand in awe of her honesty, determination, and courage. Amber does not allow her past to define her, instead she clings to God's promises and allows Him to continually guide her. She constantly seeks God's will for her life and surrenders her aspirations for His. Wherever God is leading her, she follows wholeheartedly. Amber has used every setback in her life as a stepping stone to achieve the plans God has for her life and I can only imagine the impact that the Hupomone will have on you as you turn each page. Throughout our friendship, I have been challenged to live a life saturated in God's presence and to become sensitive to the Holy Spirit's guidance in my life. I pray that you will be challenged in a similar way and to always remain in wonder of the power and presence of God."

—Tatiya Maddox

"I met Amber in 2018, in a random study group, as we were classmates in our Master of Social Work program. I honestly did not know how I felt about Amber when I met her. She stood out the most in our group of five. She seemed so grounded that I thought she knew she had it all figured out. I was on the fence about her. Fast forward to the present, Amber has been a light in my life that I had been asking God for. She is like my little, big sister, all in one. We share similar dreams and aspirations and she is one of the most dependable, determined, women I have ever met. I foresee this book allowing her to BECOME a shining light in this dark world. My forever sister, I love you and I cannot wait to see your growth and success."

—Danielle Roberts

"I tell you the truth, you have not experienced freedom until you can release what is on the heart without the worry of being judged and knowing the Holy Spirit is present. God planted Amber in my life in the middle of my college undergraduate years - Amber was a mystery to me, but something within me knew there was much to her story. Towards the end of 2018, a very turbulent time in my life, God began to birth a friendship that never would have crossed my mind. I reached out to Amber for some guidance on a mission trip to Asia I was pursuing. In her sarcastic sense of humor, she downplayed her impact while serving on these trips. This was only a representation of Amber's humility and sincerity of doing what God purposed her to do. As we both revealed parts of our lives very few people knew, we also pushed each other through the next steps, forming action plans and holding each other accountable. As you read Hupomone I pray you are encouraged to have Faith to walk through whatever obstacles life's journey presents. Amber pours out a lot of her own experiences as a testimony to this Faith. Only when we are honest with ourselves can we dwell in the Spirit of Truth. I pray you receive the revelation that you cannot do life on your own and choose to follow God's lead. No matter if you are young or old, new or experienced in Christ, lost at a crossroads in life, faced with rejection, suffered trauma, feeling emptiness, you can find yourself in Amber's shoes...or your own tattered soles."

—Johnathan Burpo

"My spirit led me to read this book ASAP, and I finished it in a day. I shed a few tears as I read through some chapters and I realized it's because this book sheds light on the true definition of Hupomone. It is an eye opener for people who are afraid of being all God has called them to be and those who are afraid of the unknown because they're worried about people's opinions. It will make you appreciate the honest people in your life because their words are necessary for your growth. May Hupomone be just that for you."

—Sacoria Lucas

"From the early stages of knowing Amber, she has always been a joy. I am in awe of the transparency in this book, as it brought tears, laughter, and realization. This book will provide hope to the many people that are faced with grief and similar hardships. It motivates you toward the purpose of who God is calling you to be. It compels you to face the covered or buried issues in becoming whole and more useful to God. It expresses that with a vow and surrendering to God, will cause us to be in places we could never imagine and it also takes us through testing for later, a testimony. I learned from this book, in life comes rejection, failures, and pain but through it all, it cultivates you for greatness and directs you to purpose. I am so excited for this book to be released because it's going to be a source for so many people in dealing with relationships, mental health, grief and identity. Also lets people know they are not alone, there is a God who cares and will help through every struggle."

—Wylisha Powell

"Hupomone is insightful, revelatory, easy to read and follow, draws you in, and will keep you wanting more. I could see myself and too felt like I was on the journey with Amber. It takes you on an emotional roller coaster, in a good way and brings with it a good balance. It allows you to not only see things spiritually but practically. Amber did a great job at explaining Hupomone and the process that it entails. Amber is an awesome story teller and the real MVP of this story is her Momma."

—Demetrius Barksdale

"I love Amber's honesty. I love how vulnerable she was in sharing her story because it takes courage. I read Hupomone in one day, and it was because of how the book flowed. I didn't want to put it down, every time I got to a point where I wanted to stop I kept going because of how engaged I was. Amber did her thing with this one."

—Johnathan Smith

"Through the years that I've known Amber, she's always been a visionary and go-getter. A lot of people say but few actually "do."; Amber does. I was in chapter 9 when I realized how much of myself I saw in her words. At times I was stupefied and just had to gather my emotions and continue reading. I connected with her words right away and through her journey I went back through my own journey. I recounted the steps I've taken that brought me to my current place. All the prayers that I prayed and even more so the prayers that were prayed on my behalf that have kept me alive and able to share God's goodness. This book is very well handcrafted and I'm thankful that God chose Amber to express herself and her experiences in only a way that she could in order to engage with anyone from any background how there will be triumphs, failures, heartbreak, unconditional love, success, and everything in between that is preparing us for God's purpose and how no matter what, His Will will prevail. Through her book, I'm for certain you will witness the strong, beautiful, God-fearing woman that I do. I hope her candor will touch your soul to help move you to a place where God wants you to be. Then you experience His greatness so that you can in turn, carry out your purpose. This book is a true diamond here."

—Alexandria Key

"Amber's story is raw and honest. But it's also full of revelation and healing. I've known Amber for some years and I have lived through some of these moments with her. However, reading the book and seeing the full story gave me a new perspective. She is resilient. You can see God's hand all over her life. There is a part of the book that will resonate with all who read. I know this book will be a blessing to others as it has been for me."

—Kahla Anderson

DEDICATIONS

This book is dedicated to...

My phenomenal parents, Momma and Daddy, for being my reason of being.

My Best Friend, Porcia Murrill, the woman whose life changed the entire trajectory of my life.

My Big Daddy, the man that taught me how to hold on to my Faith.

Mrs. Kimberly and Mr. Roddy Sanders, the people who poured into Hupomone every step of the way.

My most beautiful unborn children, my niece Serenity Grace, my Godson Grayson Eugene, and my girls in the Dominican Republic, I love you all so much.

"Lifting a person's heart, that matters. Later on in life it won't matter what car we drove, what house we lived in, or what clothes we wore. What will matter is how many lives we've touched and how many lives touched us."

– PORCIA ALEXIS-ANNE MURRILL

In loving memory of Porcia Alexis-Anne Murrill
January 1, 1993 – May 26, 2010
&
Jimmy R. Underwood Sr.
November 17, 1929 – December 10, 2018

TABLE OF CONTENTS

Introduction	1
Chapter 1 Origin	5
Chapter 2 Awakened	27
Chapter 3 Suicide	49
Chapter 4 Rejection	73
Chapter 5 Sabbatical	83
Chapter 6 Pregnant	103
Chapter 7 Humbled	119
Chapter 8 Hupomone	131
Chapter 9 Unknown	145
Chapter 10 Emptied	163
Chapter 11 Conscious	179
Chapter 12 Returning	187
Chapter 13 Beginning	199
Afterword	207
Acknowledgments	211
About The Author	218

Introduction

It was a cold Wednesday morning in the spring of 2012. The Crimson Route bus dropped me off at an unfamiliar location. I guess that's why everything around me looked so strange. I stood at the stop sign and stopped. I was used to campus being busy, bright, and loud - not still, quiet, and pale. There weren't many people walking to class; in fact, there weren't many people on this side of campus at all.

Even the squirrels were friendly on our campus, so I was confused when none ran up to me. The only thing typical about campus this day was the construction workers building something. It turns out the campus was always under construction.

Scared but hopeful, I made my way toward a small gray building. I stared at the building's two glass doors before opening them.

I didn't know what to expect, but I took a deep breath. I opened them and walked in.

As I walked down the hallway that led to the main room, I stopped and thought to myself, *"why am I here?"*

I stood in front of the doors with two decisions: I could leave or stay.

My heart was pounding.

"Sign in right here, and he will be with you in a few minutes," the receptionist with thick black hair said. I was already nervous about being there, so I just nodded and smiled at her.

Anxiety overpowered my body. Sweat from my hands stained the paper where I wrote my name, a name I no longer recognized.

Trembling, I sat down and looked around the room. The body language of each person told a story. And while life weaved our stories differently, our cry for help was the same.

How could a little gray building on the University of Alabama campus feel so cold?

I sat in my seat with a heart as cold as my fingers.

"Amber, I'm ready for you," the white man said.

The hallway leading to his office was long, narrow, and endless. A bright yellow light dangled from the ceiling, guiding us to his office.

I sat down in the chair in his office and looked at the man. The man looked back at me. We played the staring game. You know, the game where if you blink first you lose? Yeah, that game.

INTRODUCTION

My eyes wandered around the walls of his small, warm office. Anxiety said hello again.

This man, my university-appointed counselor, looked into my eyes, and sweat dripped through the crevices of my fingers. My heartbeat beat so loudly I was sure it made footprints all over my chest.

"Amber, how did you get here?" he asked me. Time ticked by, and every answer my brain tried to grab left me. I wondered the same question and more.

Do my friends know where I am? Did I get excused from English 102 to be here? For this? I'm not supposed to be here, I thought.

I couldn't answer his question because a girl like me wasn't supposed to be sitting across from a counselor like him, so I thought.

The clock said it was after nine in the morning. My counselor told me to take my time to think about his question. The problem with me taking my time is that "taking my time" led me here in the first place. Because I'd taken my time realizing I wasn't okay, I'd begun making *decisions*; and one decision, in particular, pushed me here.

With sweat dripping down my face, I gripped a white Kleenex and decided to take one more minute. When I opened my mouth to answer his question, I knew life as I once knew it would never be the same. I'd no longer be able to hide behind the pain controlling my life.

"Amber, how did you get here?" he asked me again.

"I don't know," I said. "Because the last thing I remember is leaving the guy's room down the hall from my room and waking up in a hospital."

HUPOMONE

Disclaimer: *Several people closest to me read the following pages out of love. To our surprise, the book revealed pieces of ourselves that we didn't know were still there. Seeking help was important to me, which helped save my life. I wish I could tell you how to start or continue on your personal healing journey, other than just starting, but I can't. Our journeys, our lives, were made differently for a reason. Because I'm not a licensed counselor or therapist, and this book is only my story to encourage and inspire, please know that it's okay to ask for help; don't let anyone tell you differently. If you, or someone you know, are mentally and emotionally distressed, please take advantage of the therapeutic services available. Always reach out to someone because it's never too late, no matter how far gone you may feel.*

1

Origin

I don't remember what life in the projects was like because I was two years old when we moved. But I remember everything about life in that three-bedroom, single-wide trailer at the bottom of a hill in Alabama.

Momma's room was at the far end of the trailer. My older sister, Ashley, had her own room while my younger sister, Summer, and I shared. Our room faced the main road, pointing toward the highway. We heard music from Gucci Mane, Lil Wayne, and Young Jeezy blaring from the cars driving up and down the hill at night. When we didn't hear music, we heard arguing or police sirens wailing up and down the hill.

HUPOMONE

One night in the fall of 1998, the police sirens wailed so loudly I couldn't go back to sleep. I pulled the covers over my head, trying to understand why the sirens scared me. The noise and confusion from that night made it easy for me to go to Mrs. Strawberry's kindergarten class the next day at Helena Elementary School. The school was always quieter and peaceful, and sometimes it made more sense to me when I was younger.

I made it to breakfast in time, and I couldn't wait to eat what my Momma and the lunchroom ladies had prepared for us. Momma loaded my plate with buttery grits, two crispy sausage patties, cheesy scrambled eggs, a ripe banana, and chocolate milk to wash it all down. I punched in my lunch number, and Momma's coworker told me to go through the line. Upon making my way to my usual table, I sat in my regular round blue seat and ate my food.

The bell rang, and Momma told me to throw my plate away so that I could hurry and take my Flintstones vitamins. Those vitamins always made my mouth dry, but Momma said they made us healthy. After all, she knew what was best for us.

After drinking my chocolate milk, Momma grabbed my hand and rushed me to class.

"If she gives you any trouble today, just send her down to the lunchroom, and I'll straighten her out," Momma told Mrs. Strawberry. Then Momma gave me that look of, "You better not misbehave."

Because Momma worked where I went to school, no matter what I did, she always knew about it. Mrs.

Strawberry nodded with a smile, and I straightened up and walked into the classroom.

Mrs. Strawberry was warm and kind, and her hugs made me feel like I mattered. She had fluffy blonde hair that rested below her ears and ocean-blue eyes. When she looked at me, the love in her eyes made me want to come to school. The way she kneeled and loved my classmates and I confirmed she came to work every day for us.

We did a lot in class that day, but my favorite part was arts and crafts.

"Wow, Amber," she said smiling. "You draw so well." Her rose-scented perfume hovered over me.

Drawing and writing were my ways of expressing myself, and Mrs. Strawberry always pointed out my strengths as an artist while nurturing my weaknesses. Every time she saw my work, she patted me on my back and told me how proud she was. She made it easy to listen to her. I'd always struggled with receiving compliments, so I just smiled at her and kept drawing.

"Class, put your markers inside your desks and put your books in the pouches on the back of your chair," she told us from her desk. Of course, we knew what that meant by this time – nap time. Mrs. Strawberry set the timer, flicked the lights, and we went to sleep.

My firm blue cot was closer to the door, and for some reason, my classmate, Dejuan, moved his cot right next to mine. I was confused, a state I found myself in often as I got older. I wondered why he moved so close to me, but I didn't ask him why. I stayed quiet. I was tired from the sirens the night before, and I just wanted to nap.

At first, I thought I was dreaming, but when the heat of Dejuan's breath whipped across the back of my neck, I knew it wasn't my imagination. I looked back, and he moved closer to me. He gave me a smirk, lifted my cover, and slid his hands inside my pants.

I wanted to say something, but my body wouldn't move, and my lips were tighter than a scarecrow's mouth.

It wasn't me that Momma would need to straighten out; it was Dejuan. But that was a secret I never told Momma or Mrs. Strawberry.

"Put them folders on the kitchen table and take those brand new shoes off," Momma said as she carried all her Bruno's grocery bags through the door. While Momma made it sound like she was talking to all of us, we knew she was talking to Summer and me.

Of all of my Daddy's children, my sisters Ashley, Summer, and I lived with our Momma. Ashley, four years older than me, had the brain of Einstein, and Summer, twenty-one months younger than me, had untamable energy.

More often than not, homework time resulted in Summer and me at the table. Momma first checked on our classroom behavior for the day. If our behavior chart had a sad face, a spanking was what we got. I hated being in trouble, so I did my best to make my teachers proud. But when it came to school work, I always ended up in some kind of situation.

"If Johnny has five apples and Sally takes two away, how many apples does that leave Johnny with?" Momma asked me, already knowing that my response would make her mad.

I stared at the paper, partly because I didn't know the answer. I was stubborn when it came to math because numbers didn't make sense to me and made me uncomfortable.

"Momma, can I help Amber?" Ashley asked, sitting on the couch biting her nails.

She prayed Momma would say yes because she didn't want to see me get in trouble.

While Momma said yes she could help me, a few things were certain: I dreaded homework, I didn't like math, and I hate being micromanaged.

By the end of kindergarten, I discovered I loved everything about words, language, and the arts. I also learned from Dejuan that boys wanted to touch what was underneath my clothes.

My first-grade teacher was honest and kind. In the first grade, I also met my best friend, Porcia. My second-grade teacher put up with Porcia and my sneaky attempts to get out of her class to roam the hallways and see Momma in the lunchroom. I'm convinced we were her favorite girls.

By the time I turned eight years old, though, all my childhood wonder disappeared, and I understood that growing up came with questions and fears.

I was in the third grade at Helena Intermediate School when terrorists attacked our country. I wondered if men would fly planes into my school and hurt us one day, even when we didn't do anything to hurt them. The 9/11 attacks made me skeptical of people, and I rarely made eye contact with people I didn't know from that day forward.

Ashley, Summer, and I gave Momma our Christmas lists a few months later. When Christmas Eve rolled around, Momma let us put reindeer food out for Rudolph, and we watched movies like *Home Alone, A Charlie Brown Christmas,* and *The Polar Express.* She made Ashley and Summer hot chocolate and brewed Folgers coffee for the two of us. She baked chocolate chip cookies, which Daddy always ate whenever he spent Christmas with us.

For years, Momma thought our Christmas gifts were a surprise to us, but we knew what we were getting thanks to Ashley, who'd found the gifts weeks before. Summer didn't care. On Christmas, she opened double the gifts because it was her birthday.

As a little girl, I loved Christmas. I loved the toys, but I was more excited to see the one-seat couch loaded with brand-new clothes for me. I believed Santa Claus was real for the longest time because I always got what I wanted. But it was all Momma, not Santa Claus, making sure we didn't go without.

Christmas was the one day that took away Momma's hard reality of raising three girls alone. Seeing Momma smile made me smile, and that was all that mattered.

ORIGIN

"James Span said it will be below freezing tonight, so cover the vents and the door cracks," Momma said, emotionless about the weather prediction.

Momma boiled water on the stove, and we poured it into the bathtub. After bathing, Momma laid out our pajamas and turned on the space heaters for us. Then she made a pallet on the floor so we could share body heat instead of sleeping in our beds alone. As the second-born child, I was smack dab in the middle of Ashley snoring and Summer's elbows jabbing at my ribs. Being in the middle wasn't comfortable, but it was necessary and I understood my place.

On some cold nights, Summer and I built tents with covers, books, and the ladder that once held our bunk beds together. Those fun, cold nights changed, though, when I heard rattling in the yard on two separate nights.

On the first night, I got up and peeped down the hallway to see if Momma's light had come on from the other end of the trailer. The light stayed off, so I ran back to my bed and hid underneath my covers. When the noise grew louder, I crawled to my bedroom window and saw several police officers surrounding our trailer.

"Summer! Summer!" I half-whispered, half-hissed.

She didn't budge.

Before this, a policeman approached me at school with the D.A.R.E. dog, teaching me about avoiding drugs and harmful situations. I couldn't understand why they were at my house now. I jumped back in my bed and covered my face when I heard Momma stomp from her bedroom across the kitchen floor. Sweat dripped from under my armpits, and my mouth went dry when I heard Momma yelling at them in the yard.

"He doesn't live here," Momma told the policemen, raising her voice.

The officers held an arrest warrant for my Daddy, and there was nothing I could do about it. Even though Daddy came and went, teaching me that men come and go as they please, I was his girl, and his problems became mine. I wanted nothing more than to save him from experiencing the problems that followed him all his life. I didn't understand that saving him wasn't my responsibility.

On the second cold night, I saw two white men with a truck and chains moving across our yard. Momma's feet didn't stomp across the trailer to the front door this time. I was worried. These men stole Momma's car!

I heard Momma talking on the phone the next morning, telling someone that her car had been taken. I put two and two together: maybe, Daddy had a warrant because he didn't pay child support, and Momma's car got taken because she had no money to pay the bill.

Whether I was right or wrong, "child support" became two words that haunted me from that day on.

In January, we returned from Christmas break to one of the best days of my life: career day. Momma didn't go to college. She said the kind of boys she insisted we didn't talk to kept her distracted. There wasn't much conversation about anything other than making sure we had food to eat, we were clothed, and the lights and the water stayed on, so

ORIGIN

I tuned in when a lady stepped into the classroom wearing green scrubs. A white name tag hung on her right shirt pocket, and a headphone-looking object draped around her neck.

I wanted to know what hospital department she worked in because I'd seen men and women wearing clothes like hers from pictures of my birth.

"I work for the Neonatal Intensive Care Unit at the University of Alabama at Birmingham hospital," she said to us, smiling so big.

"What that means is I take care of tiny babies," she further explained. She handed us a green pacifier half the size of a golf ball and a picture of a baby with clear plastic tubes coming from its body.

"Excuse me, nurse, what are these tubes coming from the baby?" one of my classmates asked, hanging over the silver desk.

The nurse didn't have to answer for my sake. My baby pictures looked like what she showed us. I decided right then to be a neonatal nurse when I grew up. The nurse clearly loved what she did, and I got a glimpse of the love and care the nursing staff had for me when I was a baby.

For the first time in a long time, my fears about what life would be like when I got older were replaced with the love and care that the nurse possessed for the babies she cared for.

When the recess bell rang, I met Porcia at our scheduled time in the bathroom. Today was the day I planned to ride the bus home with her. I couldn't wait to tell her about my experience on career day. I wanted to ask her what she wanted to be when she grew up, but I didn't because Porcia was brilliant. In my opinion, she'd become whatever she wanted to be.

"Did your mom give you the permission slip for my bus driver?" Porcia asked me, smiling so big that her long black curly hair got stuck in her teeth.

"Uhhhhhhh," I said, hesitant to answer because I was about to lie straight through my teeth. We had a problem. I didn't have a signed permission slip or permission from my Momma to ride home with Porcia.

"What are you going to do?" she asked me, with her head tilted and eyes glancing at me from the side, clearly upset because I didn't follow through with my part.

"It's handled", I said. All I could think about was the whooping I'd get when I got home for what I was about to do.

We did our secret handshake that Porcia made up and went back to class.

When we were dismissed from school, Porcia and I headed to the bus line. We got on the bus last, and I handed the bus driver the forged permission slip.

"Are you sure your mother wrote this?" the bus driver asked me, staring me down like she knew Momma didn't write it.

"Yes, ma'am. You can call her and ask her, and she will tell you she did," I replied, shaking and about to pee on myself because I was telling a bold-faced lie. I knew she'd call Momma because she knew her, but I didn't care.

When we got to Porcia's house, we ran to the kitchen to make marshmallow cream and peanut butter sandwiches.

ORIGIN

After we stuffed our mouths, our faces sticky and dirty, we went outside to play.

Porcia had the idea to hike in the woods behind her grandmother's home. I could see Momma, in my mind, standing at the screen door, warning me not to come back into the house with any bugs.

Hiking wasn't foreign to me either because I often snuck away to hike up the big hill in the park, behind the trailer. Being a middle child forced me to figure out what made me unique, and being outside with nature was it for me. My sisters and I were different in our behaviors. Ashley loved reading, Summer was great at numbers, and I befriended the slugs and roly-polys. I couldn't wait to put my hands in the dirt to make mud pies. Outdoors took me to a place where I felt understood, and nature's calmness gave me great ease. Any time I had a chance to play outside, I took it.

That evening, Momma picked me up from Porcia's house. Porcia's mom was one of the few people Momma trusted with me, a number so small I could count them on one hand.

"Momma, today at school, I met a nurse who made me want to be a nurse," I said, trying to see if I was in trouble for lying on her and forging her name on the permission slip.

"Oh yeah?" she asked, giving me the side-eye in the rear view mirror.

"Yes, ma'am," I said, realizing that I wasn't in trouble after all, even though Momma knew what I'd done.

Momma told me that my experience at career day was significant. She also told me the story of when I was a baby in the hospital and almost died.

"If you can't find a vein, then get somebody in here that knows what they are doing, but you better stop sticking my baby," Daddy said to the nurses, angry and hurting because his baby girl was in pain.

The medical team couldn't explain what was going on with my body to Momma and Daddy. I'd been in the hospital for over twenty days, sick and on my way out of this world. Momma said the type of pain I was in, she wished on no one.

I'd developed a meconium aspiration, which meant I had a bowel movement in Momma's womb. I breathed in the contaminated fluid, resulting in blocked airways, and making it difficult to breathe. I developed a lung infection, which blocked the fluid that my lungs needed to function. The meconium aspiration caused me to lose blood flow. A lower-extremity blood vessel pumped harmful fluid into my lungs, and a cyst formed on my right lung. As the cyst grew, I became blue in the face, and my body rejected blood flow.

"We don't think she will make it," the doctor told Momma.

Momma said she and Daddy didn't know how the doctor did it, but later the cyst was removed from my right lung, and my body adapted to breathing with one-and-a-half lungs. But things didn't end there. Three years later, the cysts returned.

"You don't hear Amber crying? Get up," Daddy yelled, kicking Momma in the shin to make her move.

"She's just hungry," Momma said and didn't move. Daddy remembered I was about to die the last time I cried like that.

Daddy jumped out of the bed like someone broke into our home, and ran to my side when he noticed my cry fading out. I was blue in the face and cold. They rushed me to the hospital in his 1990's brown Bronco.

The cyst removed three years before had returned in my stomach and formed an ectopic pancreas. The tissue connected to my pancreas grew outside of my pancreas.

The medical team removed the cyst before it could spread and cause cancer.

After Momma told me these stories, I knew I had a story to tell. I'll never forget when my third-grade teacher called me to the microphone to share it.

My class was reading our first ever written poems to our parents on this day, and it was my turn to speak.

I just stood there on the stage, trembling. I was nervous.

A pen dropped, a cell phone rang, and someone coughed.

Get it together, I told myself.

"The title of my poem is, 'This Girl,'" I said finally, my voice cracking.

I read the words without looking up, just trying to breathe, and avoid all eye contact with everyone in the audience.

I was so scared, but I read it.

"This girl is me," I ended the poem, the words tumbling out.

My teacher gave me a thumbs up, the parents gave me a standing ovation, and my classmates just stared. I'd done it. I stood in front of my entire class and shared the words that meant the most to me. God was with me, the first time of many, and I was beginning to understand that.

Momma checked me out of school that day, and I looked out the window, in silence, the whole way home.

That evening I was in the backyard again. I'd just finished making mud pies when I looked over and spotted a black and white, fuzzy worm-like creature scurrying up the stem of a green leaf. I grabbed my glass pickle jar, filled it with grass, and made a home for the creature. Before I put it inside the jar, I watched it crawl around in the palms of my hands. I didn't know what it was about this fuzzy-looking creature that intrigued me, but I took care of it. Every day after school, I checked on it to make sure it was still breathing and moving.

"You better check on that bug of yours," Momma told me one day, standing in the screen door with her hands on her hips.

What's wrong with Momma, I thought.

Momma didn't care for me playing with bugs in the backyard, so her telling me to check on my bug shocked me.

The day before, the creature crawled on the leaves. And now it was hanging from the roof of the jar in a white sack.

ORIGIN

What did I do to make it hide from me? Did I kill him? I wondered.

One day I came home from school, and it was squirming around in the sack. A few days later, it emerged from the white sack. It was an orange-winged creature with a brown tint, black lines, and three white dots on each wing. My creature was a caterpillar that transformed into a butterfly!

I don't know how that caterpillar became a butterfly, but I knew I'd have to experience uncomfortable situations like the caterpillar in its cocoon. If I remained steadfast, I'd see that my ZIP code would never stop me from being who God created me to be.

AT THE START OF MY NINTH SUMMER, I decided to get married.

"Summer, get my Bible and stand at our bedroom door. You have to be the preacher," I said. Summer grabbed my blush Bible and stood at our bedroom door.

I wrapped my white, twin-sized bed sheets around me and strapped my two-inch plastic heels on my feet. The heels were special to me because they came with a matching pair of purple stone earrings from Dollar General. These shoes were the first pair of heels I owned and the only ones Momma allowed me to play in. She was big on us not playing in our school or church shoes.

After clipping the earrings on my ears, I covered myself with the veil, a.k.a. my pillowcase. With one last look in the mirror, I grabbed the bouquet of flowers from Momma's decorative bowl and went to the hallway entrance. I stood there, smelling the musk lingering under my armpits and my legs clinging tight to each other. I was inches away from the altar, so I couldn't turn back. As I stood there waiting, holding in my pee, I noticed Summer and I had an audience – Momma, my older cousin, and my cousin's guy friend.

I'm about to get married.

As I walked down the aisle, our tight hallway, I couldn't help but wonder what I was thinking.

Amber, what are you doing? Do you even know what marriage is? You better hope nothing happens and you don't get in trouble.

"Ehhhh, Amber, I have the train, but your dress is starting to fall," whispered my cousin, who came to play that day.

I folded my dress into multiple folds just above my chest, but my heels caught on the end of the sheet. My thoughts were racing.

Amber, if this dress falls down in front of this man, you're going to be in deep trouble. Your dress doesn't need to fall. Lord, if you get me out of this one, I promise to wait until you say I can get married. I prayed to God to get me out of something I got myself into because of my wild imagination.

As I attempted to rush back down the aisle to return to my room, I fell.

I was lying face down on the floor with nothing on but a pair of panties and one shoe on my feet. At that moment, I no longer cared about having a fake marriage ceremony.

ORIGIN

I was concerned about what was about to happen to me next.

I sat there, my face streaked with tears. All I could think about was how Momma was about to be standing over me.

When my cousin and her friend left, Momma came into my room. Her black leather belt smacked my rear end. Her message came through loud and clear: *Don't play dress-up without clothes on underneath, especially when grown men are around.*

I threw my plastic heels in the corner of my side of the room, and I put on my favorite blue jeans and plaid shirt. I slid my feet into my gray New Balance tennis shoes and tied them up with rage. I threw my blue and black backpack over my shoulders and went to the backyard to be alone.

That summer, Daddy moved back in with us and took us on our first vacation ever, a trip to Florida for our family reunion.

Daddy drove well over the speed limit the whole way to Florida. Momma didn't like it when Daddy drove crazy, but she trusted him with her life and ours.

He blasted Michael Jackson's "Billie Jean" and his *Off the Wall* album, and Prince's "Purple Rain" and "Raspberry Beret," and we jammed the whole way there. Daddy loves music, and I credit him for my love for Jazz, soul music, and artists like Marvin Gaye, Anita Baker, Lauryn Hill, Musiq Soulchild, YEBBA, and H.E.R..

Music took Daddy to a different place, and I went along with him as a little girl singing, "Don't Go Chasing

Waterfalls," in his brown Bronco. Singing that song with him taught me that words in music have deeper meanings and I lived for understanding the meanings.

Daddy was one of six children. When my grandma passed away, my granddaddy became the anchor of our family. I never met my grandma, but I was told she was beautiful, a pillar in the community, and a devoted mother and servant, all roles I heard she filled with style and grace.

At the reunion, my family members told me Daddy was a Momma's boy. So when my grandma passed, when he was twenty-one, it made sense for him to look to fill the void any way he could. He didn't know her loss created a hole in him that he could never fill.

My granddaddy, a true humanitarian, preached the importance of family, God, and identifying with our roots. He led our family in prayer before we stuffed our faces with good Southern cooking and danced to the music that made us a community.

After a week of swimming, eating junk food, playing cards, and dancing in Florida, Daddy decided to cut up in a way I'd never seen him before. We were leaving the family reunion event for that day when Daddy started talking crazy in the car.

"I'll get out and walk. It don't bother me," Daddy said, eyes red and a swaying demeanor.

I knew he had a few drinks, but I didn't think it was enough to make him get out of the car in the middle of the road at a traffic light in Florida. I don't remember what ticked Daddy off, but that day I knew alcohol made him into someone he wasn't. My first time in Florida started with excitement and ended with my decision never to drink alcohol.

We returned home on a Saturday, but that didn't stop Momma from making us clean up.

"Line your clothes up by color, and get on those chores," Momma said. We put our clothes in the hallway so Momma could wash them, and we got to work on our chores.

Ashley was responsible for cleaning the bathroom and vacuuming, Summer swept and mopped, and I washed the dishes. I dreaded washing dishes and often got in trouble for having an attitude about doing them. We all dreaded doing chores, so we did our best to get them done quickly. But, when we finished, Momma made it known that the Blue Magic "grease" and the hot comb awaited us.

"Keep jerking your head like that; you're already tender-headed," Momma said as I sat between her legs on the floor, getting my hair done.

I hated getting my hair done, and having to do chores beforehand didn't make me feel any better. The slightest touch of the comb on my scalp irritated me. But Momma always made sure our hair was done, especially on Sundays.

For as long as I can remember, the voice of Bishop G.E. Patterson woke us up on Sunday mornings. As kids, going to church wasn't an option, and it meant we went to Sunday school and regular Sunday service. If our pastor preached at a special program in the afternoon, we went to that too, which meant we didn't get home until nine o'clock that night.

As a little girl, church was always interesting to me. By race, it was a true black Pentecostal church. The choir singing, "I know God is a Good God" and "Praise the Lord Everybody," drove me to join in singing every time, beating my tambourine with a smile on my face like I was in a candy store. It wouldn't be until I got older, though, that I understood the old church hymns like "Just Another Day", "Walk With Me", and "Stand By Me".

After praise and worship, our parents' gave us a dollar to put in the basket for the offering. While the pastor preached, we'd draw on the back of our parents' Bibles on the lined paper they gave us. If we stained our church dresses with ink from the markers, we'd get in trouble; our parents didn't play about those church clothes.

We loved to suck on peppermint candy during the service. But the minute we put it in our mouths, the usher, an older black lady with puffy gray hair wearing a white suit, came over with a paper towel in her hand, waiting for us to spit it out.

At the closing of the preacher's sermon, the atmosphere shifted, and church members fell to their knees on the floor, crying. They were speaking a language I didn't recognize. Many kids laughed, but I cried. At such a young age, the weight of what they were experiencing was heavy to me, and I wondered what they were feeling. I found myself often searching for more, something bigger, just something. This experience was the beginning of that *something*.

A few years later, on a warm Sunday morning, when our pastor asked who wanted to be baptized and saved, I walked to the altar. After church, he baptized me in a metal tub under an oak tree in his yard. I went under the water yearning for more, and I came up drenched in religion. I hadn't quite understood that I could never work to earn God's love, and that me having a relationship with Him wasn't based on how perfect I could be for Him.

When we got in the car to go home, my sisters looked at me and told me I'd go to hell if I listened to a particular type of music. They only knew what they heard from others, and I couldn't fault them. I knew that God was something you didn't play with, so I adopted a religious mindset based on following rules and keeping up appearances which would later cloud my ability to have a relationship with Him.

2

Awakened

In my fourth-grade class, I became the artist Mrs. Strawberry saw in me to be. I drew a bowl of fruit on a canvas in my art class that year, and my art teacher entered it into a statewide art contest. What happened weeks after she entered me into the contest shocked me.

"Amber, come to my manager's office. You need to read this," Momma said, with the biggest smile and tears welling up in her eyes. It was rare for Momma to smile like that, so I ran into the office with giddy. I wanted to know what was making her smile so big.

It was a letter from an art council in Montgomery, Alabama, letting me know that I won first place in the art contest. Because I won, they paid for Momma and me to drive there to accept my award; so we went.

I couldn't believe my eyes. The outside of the building was huge. The room we walked into was lit up like Christmas. There was a table adorned with larger-than-life checks made from poster board, and two photographers taking pictures. There weren't many people standing in the room, but it was enough to make me hide behind Momma. An escort led us to our seats, and I sank in my chair.

After the board gave us a rundown of the award, the art council presented me with my framed artwork and a fifty-dollar check, congratulating me on my work.

Much of that day was a blur. My mind was stuck on how I won an art contest like that. My first time in Montgomery ended with Momma smiling the whole way home and me using my fifty dollars to purchase sketch pads, colored pencils, and more canvasses.

I coasted through fourth and fifth grade, soaking up the lasting moments of intermediate school because I heard the horror stories about being shoved in lockers and thrown in trash cans by the older kids in middle school. Ironically, my middle school was another predominantly white school.

"School may be out, but my rules still stand," Momma said as she picked us up on the last day of school. I turned my head to look out the window and rolled my eyes.

Momma took school more seriously than my sisters and I did, which got on my nerves. She held on to those summer reading lists as if her life depended on it. To her, our lives hinged on them because she wanted us to go far.

We camped out at the library almost every day that summer. It was where Ashley memorized every word from the *Harry Potter* books. Summer dove into the *Junie B. Jones* series, and I shed tears reading *A Child Called It* and *The Lost Boy*. I don't remember what Momma checked out, but she was with us every step of the way.

While I loved reading, I couldn't wait to get home to rush to the park behind our trailer to play.

I ran to my room and took off my good shoes and threw my books on my bed. I was ready to be outside.

"Don't take those books outside, get out of those good tennis shoes, and shut my door," Momma insisted, sitting on the burgundy couch in the living room watching *Days of Our Lives*. Momma always watched that show on the black thick back television. She had a white church fan in one hand and a rag in the other. She wanted the screen door shut to keep the cool air circulating through the trailer.

Ashley didn't go outside often. Her focus was on becoming a teacher, before she decided to be a nurse. Summer and I became two peas in a pod on those long, hot, humid summer days. After all, we are close in age.

Before we made our way to the park, we walked over to the car garage a few houses down to get a few dollars from our granddaddy, who hung out with his friends there. If the ice cream man didn't come, we ran to the candy man, who lived next to us, to get pickles, Snickers, and Sprites.

Every Sunday, when we arrived at the park after church, the basketball court was crowded with young black boys and grown men. On the side of the tracks where we lived, the police were constantly rolling up on us. Often I felt purposeless by the way they looked at us. Their looks made it hard to believe that we'd ever make it out from our side of the tracks. Whether their looks meant that or not, that's how it felt.

Rap music blared from cars of the tough boys in the hood. Posted up in a demanding way on their vehicles, they'd be drinking beer and Hennessy from their red Solo cups.

"There go 5-0, time to go," one of the boys shouted, grabbing his book bag.

Summer grabbed my arm, telling me to come on before Momma pulled up. Aside from the loud music, I never knew what we'd done to get kicked out of the park, but I knew not to talk to the police; one of the boys might misunderstand our conversation.

Speaking to the police meant I was a snitch and didn't know the neighborhood code: growing up you didn't talk to the police or get caught talking to them.

Not knowing the neighborhood code resulted in my sister and me getting banged upside the head with a tape recorder by one of the boys who thought we were snitching on him. I kept my mouth shut regarding talking to people in authority from then on. I even watched how I looked at the tough boys in the hood. I didn't want my conversations with anyone to be mistaken for snitching.

"Amber, I told you to come on. There goes Momma," Summer said, upset as if I caused this.

AWAKENED

"Why are you mad at me? It's not my fault the police are here," I told Summer, ready to slap her across her face.

We knew we were on a time crunch when we went to the park. If we didn't beat the street lights home, a belt waited for us when we got there. Being outside after dark was a no-go in Momma's house.

Momma would ride up on us in the park to make sure we weren't being "fast", meaning you smiled in the face of too many men. With eyes in the back of her head and the streets, she didn't apologize. Her strictness was firm, and she didn't care if we were mad at her for it.

Momma wasn't teaching us to be strong, independent black women because she wanted to. She raised us that way because that's all she knew. That meant we became strong, independent black women.

Over time I learned that Momma wasn't mean. She was stern and had every reason to be because she technically had to raise us on her own. It took a strong woman to do that.

———

IN THE SUMMER OF 2004, Momma babysat in the neighboring town Mountain Brook, which was about thirty minutes from where we lived. She also earned extra money by selling candy, pickles, and bebops in our neighborhood. I don't know if it was the babysitting or Momma seeing the massive homes in that town, but from that point on, Momma made it her duty to drive us around the wealthiest neighborhoods to see houses and car dealerships to pick out the cars we'd like to own one day.

Momma wanted to show us that there was more to life, but I already knew it deep down in my heart.

A few days before I became a middle schooler at Riverchase Middle School, Momma talked about putting braids and beads in my hair. I spent time on Google that summer researching what middle school girls looked like, and they all had straight hair. I didn't want to begin middle school with Blue Magic "grease" smeared along my edges, so I talked Momma into letting me wear my hair straight. My crown and glory went from thick and full to straight and breaking, and I didn't care.

On the first day of school, the school bus turned into a nice neighborhood. My face rested against the window, and I gazed at all the houses we passed. These houses were much like the houses Momma took us to look at that summer and on the weekends: big, spacious, and beautiful. Even the green grass was luscious. It was a sight to see.

I got off the bus, walked into the gym, and found Porcia. Midway into our conversation, I became distracted by all the kids with cell phones and name-brand bookbags.

By the seventh and eighth grade, I understood who I was (black, thick, and misunderstood), and where I came from (the trailer on the other side of the tracks) wasn't like the average white kids at my school who wore Clarks Wallabees, Abercrombie hoodies, and Hollister jeans. Yet the black kids in my neighborhood accused me of talking "white" when I spoke "proper."

Being in the middle of those two places, I struggled to be my most authentic self. By the end of middle school, I put on two different masks to fit in, and I was exhausted from wearing them. I didn't know if I could trust people after all.

THE SUMMER BEFORE MY FRESHMAN YEAR of high school, Daddy came to the trailer one night and gave me his wallet to hold while he went out to do whatever he wanted. I love my Daddy and wanted to see him happy. So when he told me to keep his wallet that night, for whatever reason, I held it under my pillow as if my life depended on it.

Daddy was a charming man with a contagious smile and youthful high yellow skin. He had a way with the ladies, explaining why he created five of us by different women. My grandfather instilled a strong work ethic in Daddy, so he never missed work, even if that meant he was walking to get there. He had a heart of gold, too, and was unashamedly hisself. Everyone that knows him, loves him.

I knew Daddy loved Momma, but every time he came and went, Momma's broken heart showed up in how she got quiet and struggled to find happiness and trust people. She wasn't always angry, but the truth was, Daddy took a piece of Momma every time he left. But I was Daddy's girl, so I felt like it was my duty to care for him, even when he didn't take care of Momma's heart.

I had questions, though:
What would make him stay at home with us?
Why did he always choose the other woman?
Did he trust people?
Did he struggle in relationships?

HUPOMONE

What was he looking for, and did he ever find it?

Although I knew I'd never get a direct answer to these questions, because it was my job to stay in a child's place, I never stopped wondering about the answers.

"I'll be back in the morning," he told me, wearing his black cowboy boots and a black leather jacket.

"Okay, Daddy," I said, hugging him goodbye. After I heard the front door shut, I peeked out my window, wondering if Daddy would return.

I watched him walk away. I hoped he'd walk back, but he didn't.

I don't know what he loved the most, but I knew whatever it was, it was outside Momma's home.

Watching him come and go, coupled with my own relationship experiences as I got older, made me good at leaving relationships before anybody could get close to me. I struggled with relationships before I even entered one. I was scared people would leave, so I unintentionally built a wall that would be hard to tear down.

To my surprise, Daddy woke me up the following morning, asking for his wallet. I gave it to him. I was happy he was back home, even if it was only for a little while.

———

By the time I turned fourteen, the way puberty had hit me was unexpected. My hair had grown to my shoulders, my hips expanded, and my waistline was smaller. Overnight, my body became much like Momma's, and all the boys wanted me.

My sisters and I began attending parties in nearby cities, parties I looked forward to every weekend. I'd been dancing since I was eight, so by the time I turned fourteen, a girl like me could move my body in a way that brought attention. And Huey's "Pop, Lock, and Drop It" and Juvenile's "Back That Thang Up" didn't make my dancing any better. The attention I was getting exposed me to the life Momma tried to protect me from.

I don't remember many conversations about boys and dating growing up in our home because Momma didn't trust them, and I knew she didn't want us messing around. That's why I never talked to Momma about Ali, even though she already knew.

I was in ninth grade when I let Ali get close to me. I'd previously seen him in the park, and he blew my mind. I'd never seen a young man with the features of a grown man. He had chocolate skin with biceps almost bigger than my Daddy's. When he put his number in my silver LG flip phone, I smiled from ear to ear. I didn't know a thing about love, but I knew I had a crush on him.

It was a Friday night, and I sat in the passenger seat of Ali's car. I was at a neighborhood party when he hit me up to come outside. We'd moved so fast over those few months that I lost track of how I even ended up in his car. As I sat in the car with him, his muscles warmed my body, and before I knew it, his windows fogged up with body heat that clouded my judgment. I began to open myself up to that place in the world Momma told me not to go too.

His weight rested on my body, and the strength of his hands slid down the parts of me that made me a young woman. Lying there because I wanted to, attempting to understand what was about to happen, I realized I'd been there before. All I could think about was Dejuan and how he touched me.

"Are you okay?" Ali asked, his breath smelling like peppermint.

I wondered if Ali sensed the fear I had when he touched me. A fear I didn't realize took root from Dejuan.

I nodded yes.

"Are you ready?" he whispered, waiting for my answer.

The moment I opened my mouth to answer, the passenger door of his black sedan flung open, and Ashley pulled me out of his car.

"Amber, have you lost your mind?" Ashley screamed. Her face was angrier than Momma's. "You're about to make a big mistake, and I'm telling Momma when we get home."

All I could do was cry because I knew that I'd be in trouble when I got home.

That night I didn't sleep. I was afraid of what would happen when Ashley told Momma I had almost lost my virginity. I was scared and angry with Ashley because we were supposed to keep each other's secrets and have each other's backs as sisters. Whether Ashley planned to tell Momma or not, I knew I'd never hear the end of it.

I tiptoed around the house the next day, ready to tell Momma what happened with Ali. Living in fear of what could happen next was exhausting. When I got up to tell Momma, Ashley appeared at my bedroom door.

"Amber, come with Summer and me," Ashley demanded, holding the keys to her car. I didn't ask her any questions. I needed to shut up and do what she said.

As we drove down the hill to the entrance of the park, our oldest sister, Eloise, waited for us. I didn't know what was about to go down, but I knew that Eloise should be at school at Alabama State University.

Eloise was Daddy's oldest daughter. She prayed for me since I was born and always made sure to protect me.

I couldn't believe Ashley called Eloise on me. I was ready to fight because Ashley calling Eloise on me was just as bad as her telling Momma.

Eloise snatched me out of Ashley's car and hit me upside my head. As she yelled at me, all I saw were silver dots blinking in front of me.

"You better be glad Ashley saved you before you gave yourself away," Eloise said. I walked back to the car knowing this: my sisters were my best friends, and I was waiting to have sex.

―――

A YEAR LATER, ASHLEY WAS preparing to graduate from high school and planning to go to the University of Alabama in Tuscaloosa on a scholarship to study nursing. Momma got a job promotion, so Summer and I transferred to a different school. Momma was now the assistant lunchroom manager at a school in our zone, which became my new high school. Once again, I went to the same school where Momma worked. What a joy.

I knew some students who attended there because they all lived on my side of the tracks. I had friends there but I wished Porcia and some of my other friends from my other school were with me.

A few months at my new school passed me by, and on a Friday night, my sister Ashley, a few friends in the neighborhood, and myself went to a party in a neighboring city.

Ashley stopped at the local Chevron to gas up her car. While she pumped her gas, I stood outside the car to see the commotion around us. Several people stood outside their cars watching the police rush into the gas station parking lot. I saw boys from our side of the tracks run across the street into the woods. They were trying to get away from the police. We all knew what their running meant, though – someone was going to jail.

As Ashley finished pumping her gas and signaled for me to hurry and get back in the car, I couldn't help but notice the police car parked in front of us. The police lights were flashing, three policemen were standing outside their vehicles, and a young black boy was in the back seat of one of the police cars, staring right at me. He had smooth dark chocolate skin and pure beautiful brown eyes. I didn't even know this guy, let alone his name, so I couldn't understand why I got butterflies in my stomach when our eyes met.

Ashley kept telling me to get in the car so we could leave before Momma drove up on us, but I couldn't move. She started driving off, and eventually, I got in the car, still staring in this guy's eyes, and he was staring back at mine. Everything in his eyes told me he didn't belong in the back seat of that police car. But he was there, handcuffed and likely going to jail.

A few weeks later, that same guy's eyes met mine again, and this time it was at school. His name was Kree, and he was my first love.

After occasional stares in the hallway, he finally walked up to me one day and asked me for my number. This time when his eyes met mine, I hid because those butterflies returned in my stomach, and I realized it was the first time a guy gave me butterflies.

"Are we going to keep acting like we don't like each other, or will you quit playing games and give me your number?" he asked, his arms leaning up against my locker.

I started blushing and melted into my locker, my eyes getting lost in his beautiful brown eyes. I wrote my number down on a piece of paper and gave it to him. I couldn't wait for him to text me.

I don't know what he saw in me, but I knew his feelings for me had to be real because he was the only guy to ask Momma if he could date me. Momma was impressed with his boldness, and while she gave me a hesitant go, I knew deep inside she didn't want me dating him, or anyone for that matter.

Kree was the first guy I could be honest and unashamed with. I was freely myself and it felt good. He was fearless in the streets and ready to fight anyone who disrespected me. His life story was similar to mine. We both searched for ways to fill the voids we wished our fathers would fill, we didn't trust people, and we sought fulfillment from the world, not knowing it'd never fill us up. He was truly my friend.

HUPOMONE

I don't know what happened to Kree, though. He came to school one day, and everything between us changed. In fact, everything about him changed. It seemed like in a matter of minutes; he became so mean. He was getting into trouble at school and he was fighting at the parties we went to together. His love for me appeared to fade away.

He was distant. And he broke up with me out of nowhere in class.

"Hey, can you pass this to Kree?" I asked my classmate sitting in front of me. I didn't know if Kree would respond to my letter because he didn't respond to my text message the night before, or the dozen letters I wrote to him. But I watched him from the back of the classroom, hoping he would.

My heart started racing as I watched him open the letter. As he read it, I didn't know what to expect.

He got up, pulled up his sagging black pants, and glanced in my direction before he walked to the front of the classroom.

Why is he walking toward the door? What did I write wrong in the letter? I wondered.

I hoped my letter didn't make him want to leave class. After all, I only expressed how much I loved him. What was so wrong with that?

I didn't know what it was about what I wrote, but he looked in my direction one last time and threw my letter in the trash can.

I was in disbelief.

I laid my head down in embarrassment on my desk.

The bell rang, and I was too ashamed to get up, so I waited for everyone to leave. I grabbed my book bag and rushed for the bathroom when the classroom emptied.

When I came out of the classroom, Kree was waiting for me.

"We done," he said, with a cold poker face. I didn't know what to say, so I stood there. I watched Kree walk away, and he didn't look back.

I skipped my last two classes to hide in the bathroom. I sat in a stall and cried. That was the first time my heart broke.

That night, I put my headphones on and sulked through every sad song on my iPod Nano. When Daddy left, I heard Toni Braxton's "Un-break My Heart" and Deborah Cox's "Nobody's Supposed to Be Here" playing in the trailer. With Kree, I listened to Chris Brown's "Say Goodbye," Tynisha Keli's "I Wish You Loved Me," and Jazmine Sullizan's "Need U Bad." It was music that got me through the sadness I was feeling. It would always be music to get me through whatever emotions, good or bad, I was experiencing.

Our relationship and that breakup were the first time I cried myself to sleep at night. I cried as I'd never cried before. I'd mastered crying in silence, though, because I knew if Momma heard me crying, she'd have words with Kree at school and at home with me, and that was the last thing I needed or wanted.

I was too young to know exactly what love was. But, I knew what I felt for Kree was real and I was in love with him. I was willing to risk it all to save him from the pain he was feeling, the pain he never told me about, but the pain that I knew was there.

While everything in me knew I wanted to be with him and the person I knew he'd become, I also knew I couldn't beg him to stay with me. I couldn't compete with a guy who loved the streets more than me.

He'd already broken up with me, so after weeks of crying, I decided to loosen the grip he had on my heart.

I let him go, for my heart's sake.

A year later, when I was a junior in high school, another guy told me he liked me. He was tall and strong, with chocolate skin and a Colgate smile. He was four years older than me, making him a grown man. At the time, he was in the military, and every weekend he came to see me. However, my feelings for him were short-lived the day his *wife* called me.

A number I didn't know blew up my phone on a Tuesday night like I'd committed a crime.

"Is this Amber?" the woman asked, screaming at me.

"Yes, how can I help you?" I asked. She had a bad attitude, and I was more interested in knowing who she was because of the way she was talking to me. She asked me if I knew the guy, and I responded yes. After all, he was pursuing me.

"Have you been going on dates with him on the weekends?" she asked, already knowing the answer. I told her, yes, still trying to figure out what was going on.

"That's my husband," she said.

I held the phone to gather my thoughts. This had to be a joke.

"While you're on dates with him, I'm waiting for him to come back in our hotel room," she told me. I was so lost and dumbfounded that my silence made her mad. She told me to stay away from her husband and hung up in my face.

This guy was married. Married. Like exchanged vows, exchanged rings, in covenant with a whole wife, married.

I knew nothing about being involved with a married man. I was shocked. I didn't know how to feel. I started to understand why some women choose to remain single. And much like Dejuan and Kree, boys kept giving me a reason not to trust them.

I left this man alone and continued my high school life.

On my sixteenth birthday, Momma gave me her 1994 gray Maxima. Two windows were sealed with screwdrivers, holding them in place. When I put my foot to the gas, the car's entire body shook. Momma made it clear that the tires were only good for school, home, and work.

My first job came with my first car. I was flipping burgers at Whataburger. I loved working at Whataburger because it was down the street from where I lived, and it gave me financial independence to buy whatever I wanted.

I purchased black floor mats, seat covers, and a cassette adapter for my iPod Nano to play in my car with my first paycheck. I was proud of that car because it was Momma's first car and her gift to me. Momma always strived to make sure we had something to help us on our journey's in life.

HUPOMONE

I should've listened to Momma when she explained the rules for the tires. Because the day I chose not to listen to her was the same day I almost lost my life.

I was working the evening shift at Whataburger. Alabama football played in Tuscaloosa, and Auburn football played an away game, so work was slow. One of the girls on my shift called in because she didn't have a ride. Momma told me not to drive on the interstate. But if my coworker didn't come to work that day, she would've lost her job. My spirit told me that making this drive was a bad idea; it was raining, and I'd never driven on the interstate. But my heart for people trumped everything I knew and felt. I clocked out on my break and went to get my coworker.

"Thank you for picking me up," my coworker said, handing me gas money.

"Of course," I told her. I exhaled relief because I had made it safely to her house. I inhaled a prayer, pleading with God to get us back to work safely.

The rain fell in a way I'd never seen it fall before. This type of rain made Momma turn on her emergency lights when she couldn't see. And I really couldn't see in this rain.

One mile from Exit 238, the car in front of me slammed on its brakes. I tried to stop, but my brake pedal was down to the floor, and my car wasn't stopping. My wheel locked up, and my vehicle hydroplaned. We crashed into the guardrail after hitting the car in front of me.

The crash shattered the glass from my back window, pushed my trunk into the back seat, and destroyed the front end of my car. But we were safe and unharmed.

How would I explain this to Momma? I thought.

Standing on the side of the road, I called Momma and told her I'd been in a car accident. With fear in her voice, she asked me if I was okay and what had happened. After I told her I was okay and explained what happened, I tuned out because her yells from the other side of the phone told me everything I needed to know. I was in trouble, and my disobedience wouldn't live this one out.

The truth is, I'd been treading a thin line since the day Ashley pulled me out of Ali's car. My decisions behind closed doors had begun to reveal themselves in public. I was hurt. The calling on my life to empower young girls and women waged war within me. A battle between who I was (hurt, broken, and disobedient) and who I was fighting to become (whole, honest, and fulfilling my calling) was raging inside me. God was preparing me for something I couldn't see. I had no idea that a year later, life as I knew it would never be the same.

It was a warm Wednesday night in May. I sat alone on the couch watching *I Do I Did!*, a movie about a paralyzed woman put in a coma from a car accident. Her husband left her in the hospital and married another woman.

The movie was closing when some words the paralyzed woman spoke struck me.

"I don't understand God's work, but I know He does everything for a reason," she said, after waking up from her coma, remarrying her husband, and holding their brand-new baby in her arms.

I'd always heard the saying "everything happens for a reason," but for some reason, on this night, that phrase hit me like something in my life was going to happen.

That year, I began motivating my friends on Facebook with positive words. So I grabbed my phone and went to post those very words on my status. Before I could type them, *"Rest in peace Porcia Murrill"* slapped me in the face hard.

What? Rest in Peace Porcia Murrill? Surely there are two Porcia Murrill's. This headline has to be a joke, I said out loud. There was no way my best friend was dead. Porcia couldn't be dead. There was just no way.

I closed Facebook and ran outside on the porch to call Porcia. I lost count of how many times I called her and how many voicemails I left. I don't know how I slept that night, but when her mom called me the next morning, she confirmed it was true.

My best friend died.

The night before I was about to inspire others with words God intended for me.

Porcia's death will never make *total* sense to me. Her death was a pill that I couldn't swallow for years.

My clothes began to fall off; I was too upset to eat. I'd fallen into depression. I was angry with God and wanted to know why death had taken Porcia away so soon. And for the longest time, I blamed myself because Porcia lived in a way that I didn't. I wanted to know why God didn't take me instead.

That week, we celebrated Porcia's life. At her funeral, I became weak and sick. I threw up and nearly passed out. I couldn't accept it; I didn't want to. I didn't know how to.

As the celebration of her life concluded, I knew there was something more. My spirit wouldn't let up, and I wasn't going anywhere until I figured out why.

Hours later, I drove Momma's car to Porcia's home and parked across the street. I prayed for God to speak, and for a moment, I waited. I screamed so loudly for answers that the neighbors thought I was crazy.

I had questions and wanted answers. None of this was fair, and I needed to make sense

of Porcia's death.

After screaming, crying, and praying, all I had was the word *HUPOMON*. This word was on her back car tag. It was a word that wouldn't make sense, or come with revelation, for another six years...

That summer, I met Jamese, who made it known that she wasn't fond of me. She straight-up told me there was a time when she didn't like me. She knew my reputation as someone fast, wild, and stuck up, but she didn't know *me*.

Between Porcia's death, my distrust in people, and trying to make people like me, I was drained. So I didn't make it my mission to make Jamese like me. However, one conversation led to a friendship beyond people's misconceptions about me.

Jamese wasn't Porcia, but she came into my life when I needed it.

Two months passed, making it my last year of high school. At the end of the summer, my granddaddy matched the thousand dollars I saved to buy a car after a year without a car. My new but very old, white four-door Kia Sephia was six years older than my Maxima, which was an upgrade to me. It came with a cracked front windshield, a white shoestring door handle, and, much like my Maxima, an uncontrollable shake. I made wiser decisions this time because I knew this car would be all I had for a while, and I was grateful for it.

I stayed in my depression. I don't know how I won best dressed, made Homecoming Court, or got to speak at senior day. But when I cheated on my trigonometry math exam, turned it in, and then told my math teacher I cheated, I knew it was time for high school to be over. High functioning depression had a grip on me.

Aside from the parties, what kept me going was the words my granddaddy spoke to me the night he walked me down the field for homecoming court.

"Reach for the stars, baby girl," he said, squeezing my hands and standing tall in that clean suit with his hat to match. "The world is so big, and with God on your side, you can have it all, do it all, and be it all. If you don't do anything else in this life, reach for the stars, you'll make me proud when you do that. And Amber, whatever you do, don't let go of God's unchanging hands."

Then ironically, he let go of my arm when I made it to my spot on the field.

Granddaddy was right. I needed to hold on to God's unchanging hands because everything in me would need Him to survive the following year.

3

Suicide

As our pastor prayed one Sunday morning at church, I pulled out my phone to reply to a text from my friend. I didn't know Momma was standing behind me when I texted. So she reached over my shoulder and grabbed my phone out of my hands. Texting in church was unacceptable.

My reflexes snatched it back in front of all the mothers in the church. I couldn't help but wonder what in the world I was thinking. But I paid for my actions and disrespect when I got home. I guess that's why I found it interesting when Momma sadly told me to take a seat across from her, in the living room, a few hours later.

I took my seat as she looked at me, staring me down with sadness in her eyes.

Momma showed sadness when she wanted to give us the world but couldn't, or when Daddy hurt her. Daddy wasn't staying with us anymore, so I knew it was something Momma wanted to do but knew she couldn't do.

Momma made several comments that year about how she wanted me to go to college, as Ashley did, but she couldn't afford to send me, so I assumed this was that conversation.

I was right.

"I don't have the money to send you to school," Momma said, holding back the tears.

I needed a college to give me some scholarships if I wanted to go anywhere. I was smart, but beginning to search for myself in middle school and high school, I lost sight of how important my grade point average was to earn a scholarship.

"I know," I told her, knowing she felt terrible for what she wanted to do but couldn't.

Momma's face grew tight, and tears welled up in my eyes. Seeing Momma give so much of herself all of those years made me want to give her more and going to college was that start for me. She wanted us all to have a life that surpassed the cards life dealt her, but she knew it came with a cost she couldn't pay.

I sat there in silence, my body stuck to that one-seat couch I loved seeing on Christmas day.

I was hot, burning up. I was emotional.

SUICIDE

We sat there staring at one another, not having anything to say.

She taught us to be strong and push through when life got hard, so I didn't let a tear fall from my eyes in front of her.

"It's okay," I told Momma and walked back to my room.

I sat on the edge of my bed in silence. Momma muted the television in the living room, listening to hear if I cried. I didn't know if it'd be okay, but I stood on the idea that it would.

I had no idea what life would look like beyond high school, but I wanted better. I knew in my bones that I was college-bound, but aside from student loans, I didn't know *how* to get the money to go. I was scared about my future but I got up and hoped for the best.

I developed a routine that summer. I got promoted to team leader at Whataburger, so I committed to working fifty-plus hours on the graveyard shift. When I got off work, I browsed the internet for scholarships. I called several organizations offering scholarships, and I met with anyone willing to meet with me. I committed to this plan because I'd decided to step out on faith and apply to two colleges: Auburn University at Montgomery and The University of Alabama in Tuscaloosa. I received acceptance to both.

The work I put in paid off because scholarship money from everywhere began to roll in. I had a choice to make on which college I'd attend.

It would've been logical for me to go to the college that offered more scholarship money, but my spirit told me to trust God and go to The University of Alabama (UA).

My university student account sat in the negative for weeks that summer. As I worked and waited for more money to come in, I found my roommate. We were in the same boat but believed God for different things. I wasn't alone.

I knew I was crazy for believing God wanted me to go to UA, partly because I wasn't an Alabama football fan and didn't have all the money for the tuition. But as I worked and waited, Momma latched onto my faith. She knew there was money out there, so she began making calls.

In the meantime, we chose the cheapest dorm room and meal plan. Even with going for cheap, my student account was still in the negative the week I left for school. What trusting in God looked like was what He was teaching me. While I didn't know how I knew I was going to UA because what God was about to do in my life was more important than the degree I'd get. And I waited to see how.

Low and behold, Momma had done it again. Those calls she made cleared my student account, and I left my hometown for Tuscaloosa, Alabama.

In August 2011, Momma, Daddy, Summer, my grandma, and I rolled up on one of the biggest campuses I'd ever seen. I didn't go on a school visit to UA because I knew that's where I was supposed to go, and a few years prior, we moved Ashley into her dorm room there.

I was quiet in the car while Momma and Summer were on cloud nine. Daddy became a different man on that campus. His love for Alabama football came close to his love for his children. My grandma was smiling big. Ashley was at her apartment and she waited for me to arrive.

I didn't have time to gaze at the place I'd call home for the next four years because the unloading crew immediately opened my door and welcomed me.

"Roll Tide," one of the guys yelled, unloading Momma's SUV and the U-Haul Daddy rented for the day.

Momma bled that Auburn Tiger orange and blue, which explains why her eyes got big, and she let out a snicker, saying, "Lord have mercy" when the guy yelled Roll Tide.

Daddy was smiling big and let out a loud "Rolllllll Tiiiiide." All I could do was laugh.

In less than ten minutes, I was unloaded and sent on my way.

I walked inside one of the oldest residence halls on campus, which explains why it was so cheap. Rose Towers was a lofty, brown, thirteen-floor building with a flat top. It was dreamy, to me, in size but creepy on the inside. It overlooked a river, and on the other side of the river were these big houses that lit up the night sky, much like the houses Momma took us to see when we were little girls. It was all a dream turned into reality.

I traded my completed information card for a set of keys to my room on the ninth floor. As I made my way to the elevator, several members of the housing staff yelled "Roll Tide," the official greeting of UA. I'd never experienced anything like this. It was hilarious.

HUPOMONE

I got off the elevator and walked to my room, where my roommate waited for me. We lived in a one-bedroom suite with a kitchen, living room overlooking the river, a box-sized office (which became our makeup room), and a bathroom. Sharing wasn't new to me because Summer and I shared a room until my sister left for college.

The resident advisors unloaded my belongings out of the cardboard box and into my room, and Momma, Daddy, Grandma, Ashley, and Summer said goodbye to me.

Life for me at UA began.

The following week, my roommate and I set out for the university's Week of Welcome (WOW), a huge event that welcomed new students to campus with several different events throughout a week's time. We signed up for any student organization we believed fitted who we were as young women, and we left with bags of free stuff. Ashley was big on me getting involved on campus and starting the semester off strong, so WOW was mandatory for me.

Afterward, we made our way to the Capstone College of Nursing, where we registered for the class.

I couldn't believe it. I was a student at The University of Alabama.

Porcia was gone, and Jamese attended college at Jacksonville State University, so I wanted to make friends. A few of my friends from home came to school with me, and within a semester, I found more friends, one of those friends being Brooke.

SUICIDE

"Hey, are you Nyla?" Brooke asked, standing in the fried chicken line, smiling with her long dark hair and long chocolate legs.

"No. My name is Amber," I told her, pausing and interested to know who Nyla was.

"Oh, I'm sorry. You look like this girl from back home," Brooke said, still smiling, not showing the slightest bit of embarrassment. She was comical and giddy. Our accidental encounter wasn't an accident at all.

Who I surrounded myself with was important because those relationships determined who and what I'd become. Each friendship was significant because each woman represented hope and strength in numbers for me. While I continued to work through the pain from losing Porcia, these women were the newness I allowed in my life for the first time in a long time.

I tried my best to dodge the freshman fifteen bullet, but it shot me right in the thighs and butt, making me thicker than I already was. My dorm room next to Lakeside Dining Hall didn't make it any better. On Sundays, it served my grandma's style of Southern cooking. The fried chicken and cornbread went exactly where Momma said it'd go on my body and my pants went up in size.

Football in the South is a big deal, but it was an even bigger deal at UA. I eagerly anticipated football season, but not because of the games. I didn't even understand football. Football season meant payday every week for me. Many students were willing to pay hundreds of dollars to get their hands on football tickets. I never asked for this much money, but they offered it to be in that stadium. I inherited my hustler trait from my Momma and my Daddy, so I sold mine weekly, and I set aside my profits from the tickets for bills.

I no longer lived under Momma's roof, and this newfound freedom reminded me that I was growing up. I thought I was "grown." I didn't have a curfew anymore and I didnt have to answer to an authority figure. I was my boss, but would I make the right choices? My heart had been empty since Porcia's death. How could I make wise decisions in this state?

―――

IT WAS A FRIDAY NIGHT WHEN BROOKE, another friend, and I went down the hall to a room for a kickback. Kickbacks were similar to parties, except they had fewer people and a chiller atmosphere. My friends didn't know, but I used this kickback to cope with my depression.

I vowed years before never to drink alcohol because of what I'd seen it do to Daddy. But on this night, my first time drinking, I threw those shots of Hennessy back like I knew what I was doing. Juvenile's "Back That Thang Up" came on, and I stood on the boys' room table, gyrating my body; my friends wondered what was wrong with me.

The room got hot and stuffy, and everything started spinning. Either I'd gotten too hot, or the alcohol-impaired my judgment because my clothes started to fall. The alcohol masked all the pain living inside me, and I laughed.

SUICIDE

I was brought back to reality when a guy named Ty, and my friend, pulled me off the table and carried me to my room.

Ty took me to my room, while my friend went to find Brooke and brought me water and a warm towel. I laid there in my bed with Ty sitting right next to me. Because of his kindness, Ty restored and changed how I viewed men for a moment. Instead of taking advantage of me, he covered me up in my most vulnerable state.

The following day when I sobered up, I had one thought: I was no better than Daddy the night he got out of the car at the traffic light in Florida, drunk.

When I returned from Christmas break to start my second semester, I realized what I wasn't dealing with in private -- depression -- was showing up in my life in public - getting drunk to cope with the pain.

I reached out to Jamese and told her I wasn't okay. Jamese connected me with her best friend, Sophia, a sophomore at UA.

Sophia told Jamese that she was sure I was a great girl, but she didn't have the time to be there for me. She was honest in the most loving way, but the words hurt. I'd mustered up the courage to admit that I wasn't okay, only to feel like my well-being didn't matter.

Sophia couldn't invest in me, though, because of her grief for a friend who died in the same residence hall the year before I moved in. When she became an RA, she asked to be in any building but mine. But there she was, in the same residence hall as me.

A few days later, Sophia invited me down to her room. I was shocked. Although she had a smile that welcomed love and community, it was hard to open herself up to someone when dealing with her own stuff.

I sat in the corner of her room, my heart pounding like I was sitting with Momma.

We had a casual conversation that evening, and I left her dorm room, not knowing when we'd connect again. To my surprise, a few weeks later, our paths crossed, this time in a way neither of us expected.

"Amber Underwood, please press one to accept this call from the Shelby County Jail," said the automated voice.

Who'd gone to jail? Why were they calling me? I wondered.

I pressed one.

"Amber, it's me, your Daddy," Daddy said from the other side of the phone.

I began to cry.

"Daddy, why are you in jail, and how did you get there?" I asked him, hurting inside without knowing the facts.

He told me he was in jail for not paying child support. My mind flashed back to when the police surrounded our trailer. *When would child support stop haunting me?* I wondered.

Later that evening, Daddy was released from jail. I was happy but also hurting because I realized I carried the problems of others, in addition to mine, and I didn't know how to handle them.

SUICIDE

The following Sunday, I went to church with Ashley looking for another reason to live. She dropped me off at Lakeside Dining Hall when church service was over. I got my usual Sunday dinner – fried chicken, macaroni and cheese, collard greens, and cornbread. While I was dressed in Sunday's best, I wasn't at my best. But when Bradford yelled my name, somehow, he put a smile on my face.

"Aye yo, Amber," Bradford said.

"Hey," I said, fake smiling because I was ready to get back to my dorm room.

Bradford was friends with a few guys in my dorm. He had a heart of gold, loved people, and sang as he walked.

"The guys and I are having a little kickback in our room tonight, and we want you and your girls to swing by," he said, with his arm around my neck, showing nothing but teeth.

"Uh, I'll see what the girls are doing and let you know," I responded, hesitant to go because all I could think about was my behavior from the kickback I attended a few weeks prior.

"Hey, actually, we'll be there," I told him after thinking about it. After I turned around to head back to my dorm room, Bradford said my name one more time.

"Amber, remember 'we're just ordinary people, we don't know which way to go and cause we're ordinary people, maybe we should take it slow,'" he sang, a few of John Legend's actual words and a few words I didn't realize I'd never get to hear him sing again.

Bradford didn't know it, but I didn't know which way to go. My faith in God had begun to waver.

HUPOMONE

I made it my mission to uphold an image that made it look like I had it all together, even if it meant I was dying inside. I'd been depressed since Porcia died. This depression, coupled with Daddy's arrest and unpaid tuition, left me isolated.

That night I sat on the couch in the guy's room, laughing, smiling, and having what appeared to be a good time. I wanted to be there, and I needed to be there. But I wasn't there.

No one could see the pain inside me on the surface, but that's how depression worked for me. Others didn't see the signs or the tears. No one else felt the weight. I hoped someone would find me when I felt lost. How could I be in a room full of people yet somehow still feel alone?

The music blared. A basketball game was on TV. Everybody was laughing, but I sat on the couch, hurting and fading away.

They were all busy doing their own thing, except one of the guys who locked eyes with me all night. The air conditioner was loud, and my thoughts grew louder with it. I told myself repeatedly I wanted to be there, and I had to be there. I just had to be there.

I laid my head on the arm of their couch, choosing to rest my mind. It didn't work, though. I wanted to be alone.

I got up and walked to the door.

"I'm going to sleep, guys," I told them, crying inside and hoping someone would see my pain.

"Where are you going, girl?" Bradford asked me. Everyone was looking in my direction, especially the guy who had locked eyes with me all night. I knew the guy

SUICIDE

wanted me to stay, I knew they wanted me to stay, but my mind was telling me to leave.

"I'm tired," I told Bradford, because I was. They told me they didn't want me to leave, but they understood that I needed to rest.

I walked out of their room and let go of God's unchanging hands, the very hands my granddaddy told me not to let go of as he walked me down the field for Homecoming Court.

I walked down the dark hallway with two of my closest friends – isolation and depression. Isolation held one hand, and depression gripped the other. Loneliness already lived in my mind, and grief rested in my soul. I became these: isolation, depression, loneliness, and grief. They had a hold on everything, so that I couldn't think clearly. They made sure they asked me their questions, and I answered them because they were the ones who listened to me that night.

Do you really think they wanted you to stay? Do you really think they care about you? Why do you want to live? Why do you keep getting back up every time you fall? Do you think God sees you and hears you? Do you think you have a purpose? And will it be successful? Who do you think will miss you?

They walked me to my bedroom door and disappeared.

I stood face-to-face with a door that led to life or death. I committed suicide in my mind before my feet walked through the door.

Sophia was the resident advisor on call that night. She'd just completed her rounds when she came back to her room to see one of my friends beating on her bedroom door, begging for her to come and help me. By the time she got to the room, Brooke had picked the lock to my bedroom door, trying to get in. They couldn't open it, so they busted down the door to get to me. By the time they both got to me, I wasn't myself. My life was slowly fading away.

Sophia held me in her arms, and Brooke saw me that night in a way no one else had ever.

A few hours later, I woke up in the hospital.

"She doesn't know where she is, and she may not seem like herself when you go in there, but it's important that you be strong," said the doctor, standing outside of my room.

I heard every word. The room was windowless with gray walls, cold and empty, just like me. I hid my face behind the white sheet that covered my body, trying to make sense of the night.

I shivered. I was thirsty. I wanted someone to explain why I was in a room that wasn't like the typical hospital room.

I was locked in.

The doctor came into the room and explained that I'd attempted suicide that night, and Brooke and Sophia found me. He told me my friends, family, pastor, and the first lady were there to see me when I was ready.

Momma and Daddy entered my room first.

Momma cried, and for the first time in my life, I watched Daddy wipe tears from his eyes. I knew their tears took the place of the words they wanted to say but couldn't. I heard every word they couldn't verbalize.

My pastor and first lady came in and prayed over me, and Ashley came in after them. Not everyone in the lobby came in to see me that night because some couldn't make it past the door.

When those who did come into the room left, I sat in silence, catching my tears in my hands. Porcia's death, in conjunction with other things life had thrown at me, almost led to my death.

Life wasn't supposed to be this way.

While everything in me wanted to die that night, everything told me I needed to live. I had to live but I needed to get help.

I was released from the hospital the next day. When Momma and Daddy dropped me off at my dorm room and left, I sat in shame in the middle of my living room floor. How would people perceive me when I walked the hallways of Rose Towers? That didn't matter, though. I shamed myself before anyone could shame me.

I carried shame everywhere I went. I was so fragile that my entire body may have broken if I'd tripped. Walking into a room full of people made me cringe, and I felt like every person that looked at me was judging me, even if they weren't. I needed an outlet to release what I felt, so I started working out again.

The first morning I was ready to go to the gym, I heard a knock on my door. Looking through the peephole, I saw a white guy, someone I'd never seen before.

I opened the door and said hello.

"Is Amber Underwood here?" he asked me, wearing a smile that I wasn't.

"I'm Amber," I told him.

"This is for you," he said, handing me a white sealed envelope marked "CONFIDENTIAL" in bold red letters.

I said thank you, he left, and I closed the door.

I stood there sweating and shaking.

I tore through the envelope in fear. This envelope represented one more thing to stress about, and I didn't want to be in trouble.

The words on the inside went something like this:

"Amber Underwood, this is blah blah blah blah blah. It is the University's creed to ensure that the well-being of each student is our number one priority. Please report to the counseling center on Wednesday, blah blah blah at a quarter to nine. Thank you, and we look forward to meeting you."

Boom! Just like that, an official notice had been signed, sealed, and delivered to me. However, it was up to me to go with my truth, where I believed I should never go - therapy.

Wednesday morning, I went to the Counseling Center. I signed a name I could no longer recognize because while I was trying to deal with my pain, I lost myself.

I sat down where the receptionist told me to sit. A white girl with long brunette hair sat next to me. I should've been comfortable sitting next to her because we both were in the same place, but I was uncomfortable.

SUICIDE

"Why are you here?" she asked me. I just looked at her and shrugged my shoulders. Letting someone into my life at such a time like this scared me. Besides, the real question was, why was *she* here?

I think she was reading my mind because when she noticed I wasn't saying much, she kept talking to me. I couldn't understand why she was so comfortable with me.

"I'm here because I need help," she said confidently. I wanted to know what she needed help with, but I didn't want to ask. She noticed I wasn't going to say anything, and once again, she told me more about herself.

"I thought about hurting myself a few weeks ago," she said. My eyes got big, and once again, I stared at her and just listened. She told me a lot in those few minutes, but what stood out the most was how we weren't different from each other, after all.

In my eyes, she had everything I didn't have. Our socioeconomic statuses were different, but we both believed we didn't need to seek help when we needed it the most.

Before responding to her, a man from the end of the hallway called out for me. So many thoughts swirled through my head.

The last time I walked down a hallway like this, I headed for an end with isolation and depression. I was feeling all the feels.

As I made my way to the end of this hallway, I gave the girl one last look. What she said to me next struck me to my core.

"Amber, purpose comes when you admit that you need help," she said, with hope for my life in her eyes.

I walked into the man's office and got help.

I sat on a chair, looked at the man, and the man looked back at me. We played the staring game.

My eyes wandered around the walls of his small, warm, cozy office. I was so scared, but I needed to be there.

I'd never been to counseling, and no one ever told me not to go. Seeking professional help just wasn't talked about in my community. Solely praying about it was the solution. Adults also told us never to tell anyone our business because what goes on in-house stays in-house. I guess that's why I was hesitant to open up.

I didn't need to be diagnosed with depression because I knew I was. I was also spiritually depressed, the kind of depression where you want to hear from God, but you don't feel like He is near.

I was in the right place.

"Amber, how did you get here?" the counselor asked.

"Can I have a moment?" I asked. He gave me a moment to think.

I couldn't answer his question because a girl like me, who was supposed to be strong and have it all together, shouldn't have been sitting across from a counselor. Instead of counseling, I should've been somewhere helping others. But how could I help someone else when I wasn't okay?

Suicide and depression can be tricky because the signs are subtle. Isolation took me to a place and tormented me with questions about who I was and whether my life was worth living. Anxiety had me bound, and fear crippled me. I was on the battlefield with them in my mind. I was

SUICIDE

fighting for my life mentally, and they almost won the battle physically. I knew they didn't belong, and I had to make sure they didn't remain in my life. I had to remember something, anything that was worth living for. It was hard, but after I identified what was worth living for – God loving me and keeping me, my family, and my purpose - I stood face to face with them and told them to leave.

I needed to start with his question to begin healing. As I took another minute to think about how I'd answer him, I remembered what the girl I'd just met said. She was right. Purpose comes when you admit that you need help, and I needed help. I wanted help.

"Are you ready to tell me why you're here?" he asked me.

"I'm ready," I said, my hands more wet than when I first came in.

I was ready to do the work, no matter how long it took.

I told the man everything to know about me so that he could give me the practical tools to begin healing.

I said hello to my journey to healing.

In February, I got an email from my Human Development 101 professor, Kimberly Sanders, letting me know she prayed for me and thought of me.

Mrs. Sanders reminded me so much of Mrs. Strawberry. She wasn't short like Mrs. Strawberry, but she had ocean-blue eyes and big blonde hair that rested below her ears. From the first time we met, I could tell there was a genuineness about her love for me, making it easy to be my most authentic self: disciplined, honest, human, gentle, and resilient.

I don't know what made me ask her for prayer one day, but I did, and she became a constant in my life, reminding me of the importance of allowing myself to yield to God and what each season of my life was trying to teach me.

She sent me an email two months before I tried to commit suicide, reminding me that God was working in me and I'd see the promises if I allowed myself to do the work with God. She added that she wanted me to know that God would be victorious in my life and that I needed to claim that victory. With humor, after telling me that I was admired and loved by her, she told me she was starving, and I could do nothing but laugh because our fast metabolism made us more alike than we thought.

I WAS HIRED BACK AS A TEAM LEADER at Whataburger in the summer. Switching between the morning shift and the graveyard shift was exhausting. Boiling the gunk out of fryers weekly, serving burgers, and doing my best to be a leader was hard. But I was doing what I had to do. I sacrificed my summer, that should've been spent with my friends, to scrub drains and pinch pennies to make sure I had enough money for school expenses.

I knew I'd start back at UA in the fall, but I didn't know how I'd pay for it again. It would've been wise not to go back, but God was still doing work in me and that work had to take place on that campus.

The previous spring semester, I applied to be a resident advisor. I wanted to make a difference in students'

SUICIDE

lives across campus, as my resident advisor did for me, and this was a way for me to do it. And having my housing paid for would also mean I could come back to UA. My faith was growing, so I rested in the waiting.

While resting in the wait, I received an email from Housing and Residential Communities telling me I was wait-listed for the resident advisor position. I didn't know how any of this was going to play out, but I was going to learn *Who* (God).

After a long Thursday twelve-hour graveyard shift at Whataburger, I drove my shaky car up to my grandfather's rocky driveway. White dust was flying everywhere, and I saw him on the porch in the distance. His house was where my family gathered for traditional holidays and family events. My grandfather was full of wisdom so going to see him whenever I could was easy. He made conversation safe.

He sat in his rocking chair, rocking back and forth, sipping cold water from his clear glass.

I sat next to him.

The summer air was rough, and I smelled like grease sitting in the chair next to him. I guess he sensed something was troubling me because he looked at me and told me to tell him what was wrong.

"I don't know how I'll go back to UA this fall," I told him, talking with my head down and my nose getting a whiff of the grease staining my shirt.

"Pick your head up and tell me what you need," he said, grabbing his wallet. "I can't help you if you don't tell me what you need." My grandfather was big on us holding our heads high.

I'd be lying if I said asking him for money that day didn't bother me. I was still learning how to ask for help, and I didn't want to need anyone's help, but I did.

"I'm going to give you this money, but I believe God is going to show up, and when He does, I want you to call me," he said, smiling and handing me the check. He was confident in what he believed, and I latched on to his faith like Momma latched on to mine when I first left for UA.

A few weeks later, Whataburger awarded me a scholarship I received every year until I graduated from UA. My boss cut me a check for two consecutive semesters without knowing anything about my situation. With that assistance and some assistance from my aunt and uncle, I returned to UA, moving into Bryce Lawn apartments with Brooke and my roommate from the previous year.

A week after I moved into Bryce Lawn apartments, I received a call from the Presidential Village community director, asking me to come in for an interview for a resident advisor position. As I walked from Bryce Lawn to Presidential Village, all I could think about was my granddaddy's words a few weeks prior – "I'm going to give you this money, but I believe that God is going to show up and when He does I want you to call me."

I called my granddaddy right after the interview and told him he was right; I'd gotten the job as a resident advisor in Presidential Village.

God had done it again. I was mind blown and couldn't hold back the tears.

I later learned that the money he gave me, before I gave it back, was money Daddy borrowed from him to pay

SUICIDE

for my tuition that semester. Momma, my Granddaddy, and Daddy were all clinging to faith with me. They believed in me.

I tried to wrap my mind around how I stood and lived on those grounds as a resident in Rose Towers, not even six months before this.

How was it that that very building got torn down in the same year I tried ending my life? How was it that after its destruction, in that exact location, a new building was built and I was a resident advisor in it? How was it that when I returned to UA, I wasn't sure if I'd be there longer than a month, but I was? None of it made sense.

God told me to go back, even when those nearest me doubted the move. God told me to go back, even when my student account was in the negative. God told me to go back because He was doing something that no one could see at the time.

I bloomed on those very grounds imperfectly for four and a half years. What I'd gone through qualified me and pushed me into my calling.

But how is it that I said yes to God, to myself, and still got rejected?

4

Rejection

I HAD IT ALL PLANNED OUT. I'd get into one of the top nursing schools in the state, become a neonatal nurse, go on a mission trip, get married, and travel the world, in that order. It was simple to me, and those plans gave me security and direction.

I was tunnel visioned, giving it my all. I wasn't working hard just for me. I was doing it all for those who came from my side of the tracks. I wanted them to know there was a world to see, and I needed them to know they could see it.

As I pursued this path, a path I created for myself, I picked up traits that began molding me. Being a resident advisor allowed me to build relationships with students, learn how to design programs, handle emergencies, and work with university administration. I learned how to juggle multiple hats working in housing. However, the most significant experience of them all was leading my first residence hall small group.

I didn't know what I was doing, but I longed for community and people who understood me. I knew other women wanted community too, so I made it my mission to help create the space for connection.

That Fall, three other women and I opened the doors of the seventh floor in Presidential Village for women from all over campus to join the small group. I envisioned a few women opening their hearts to being in our small group because, let's face it, girls and groups can get catty if not handled with love and care. I was surprised when over fifty women walked through those double doors, seeking what I'd been praying for - a place of belonging, a place to be fed, and a place to grow.

Listening to some of those women's stories showed me how important it is for people to have a place to be themselves without judgment. I was thankful to be part of a team of women who wanted to be in that place.

After two hours of eating and explaining our goals for the small group, several women officially joined our small group, and we *promise*d to be a safe place for them.

While I know we had a significant impact in some of these women's lives, months later, it became clear that leading others comes with great responsibility, a responsibility I wasn't ready for like I thought I was.

Under my leadership, the way I led and cared for those women was observed by members who were a part of the

REJECTION

group and by many who weren't. It was through leading others that my leadership skills were challenged and my character was pruned. When I sat down to learn from my mistakes, a year later, the door to lead women, by myself, opened itself up to me again.

It's one thing to learn about yourself on a private level. But when God tells you to sit down and deal with what may be your downfall, publically, it hits differently. The start of my downfall was how I perceived my hair. God told me to start with transitioning back to the nappy hairstyle I had before I entered middle school.

To me, I never looked so unattractive in my life. Transitioning my permed hair to its original thick natural state was more complicated than people could see. I dreaded going to class because I didn't feel like myself. My twist-outs weren't cooperating, and I just wanted to cry. I'd placed my worth in my hair and didn't even know it.

Middle school proved to me that looks are important, so I was faithful to my extensions and sew-ins to make sure I looked the part. When my hair needed a trim, I cut it myself. I was fearful of it not growing back, and going natural was already asking too much of me. So when those white boys rolled up on me that night and shouted some words I'll never forget, I had a moment where I questioned who I was as a black woman.

Late one Friday night, I walked back to my dorm from Lakeside Dining Hall, carrying a late-night snack. The only thing I focused on was getting back to my room to eat and hide my hair.

As I made my way across the street, I saw a black four-door Ford F-150 speeding up to me. It appeared the truck wasn't going to stop. I ran across the crosswalk as fast as I could, hoping I wouldn't drop my food or coffee.

Shaking, I made it to the stop sign on the other side of the road.

"Get out the road, you nigger," the white boys shouted at me, flying the American flag on a pole connected to their truck. The butterflies in my stomach started flying, and my face got hot. I was anxious. I stood there in disbelief; things I thought I knew about people, this university, and life was the polar opposite.

Being raised in a predominantly black neighborhood and attending a primarily white school for most of my life, I learned to adjust to both worlds, even though I'd never fully adjusted to the ways of one of the worlds.

I was never one to talk about race and the social injustices surrounding me as a black woman or a black person. Not because I was scared or the conversation made me uncomfortable, but because my experiences growing up were different. But on this night, with those four white boys, a tight feeling swept over me, and I was furious and sad. I needed to process this experience.

I wasn't just black to those white boys: I was inferior to the white race. I was a "nigger" to them, so who I was on the inside didn't matter to them.

Their behavior was a difficult adjustment for me because the reality of who I am as a black woman was a distaste, or intimidation, to some guys who knew nothing about me. Were these white boys to blame for the words they spoke? Of course. But who else was at fault here?

REJECTION

We learn values and principles from somewhere, from someone. Those boys *learned* to call me a nigger, something I'm not.

Belief in false and degraded teaching means the misled person uses words that bring death, and not life. People who believe untruths become something they never intended to be in the process. And unless the teaching is willingly and openly unlearned, wrong teaching and believing is how generation after generation suffers from racism.

Between experiencing that racism was alive, learning that my character needed developing, and feeling unattractive through the transition of my hair, I couldn't wait to get home that summer. I packed all my belongings and went home to work at Whataburger.

THE SUMMER AIR WAS HUMID AND HOT. My Kia Sephia started acting up. When it didn't run, and Momma worked her second job, I walked to work. To walk to work when I had to didn't bother me because I saw Daddy do it when he had no way to work. It was normal for me. We did what we needed to do to get to where we needed to go. I did what I had to do.

Momma was off work on a Wednesday morning, so I drove her car to my summer classes at a local community college. I took classes to increase my chances of getting into nursing school at UA. My plan was working, and so was I. But all the security I had in my plan began to fade when Momma called me to tell me I'd received a letter from UA.

"Amber, your letter from the Capstone College of Nursing is here. Do you want me to open it?" Momma asked, sounding so happy over the phone. I knew she was delighted because deep in her heart she knew I'd gotten into nursing school. She wanted my dreams to come true just as bad as I did.

I was driving home from class and anxious to know, but I wanted to open the letter, so I told Momma to wait for me to get home.

That drive home was rough. I couldn't think straight. My hands steered the wheel, and my eyes were on the road, but my mind was everywhere. This letter wasn't just any ordinary letter; my future lay in the hands of the words printed on the paper.

When I got home, I said a prayer, took a deep breath, and opened the letter.

"Denied."

I'd been denied admission into the nursing program.

"Denied?" I was so confused. Denial wasn't part of my plan. I couldn't understand what was happening and how it happened.

My breath caught in my throat. My hands started to shake. My mind began churning out new plans - ways to correct this mistake, classes to take next, ideas to pay for all this. I met and exceeded the program requirements. I'd become involved on campus, built my resume, and kept my grades up. *What did I do wrong?* This moment destroyed my thinking of how life was supposed to go.

REJECTION

What else can I do? I questioned.

I'd placed my hope in what I achieved and created an idol out of what should add value, not define me. I credited every open and closed door to my accolades. My accolades became my identity.

I questioned my worth because I couldn't understand how I said yes to God's plan and still got rejected. I was tired of going through the motions of feeling like my back was against a wall that would never fall. So that evening I drove to church and sat in the parking lot to talk to an old friend.

I was in tears, trying to understand how this happened to me and why it happened. My friend held me and listened as I spoke, and when I finished, he looked at me and said some words I'll never forget.

"Amber, God honors our desires, but He won't honor what He isn't calling us to," he said. "I need you to hear me. God is calling you to a life where you'll have to make some sacrifices, but they shouldn't kill you."

I sat there shell-shocked and unable to move or speak. I didn't know what my friend knew or how, but I knew he was right.

I thanked him, even though I was still confused about what was next for me.

There was no clear road map guiding my next step. I'd *written the plan and made it plain*, then defaulted to feeling like God abandoned me. My desire to make it out of my neighborhood was taking me out. I was determined to make my plan happen, so I retook classes to boost my grade point average even higher. I was drowning in student loans.

HUPOMONE

On the following Friday, I stopped by Eloise's salon to get my hair done. The smell of shampoo and shaving cream was so strong they could've slapped me in the face. I walked on black hair that fell from men's heads getting fresh for the weekend. Chemicals and heat reminded me of when Momma bathed my hair in Blue Magic "grease," followed by the hot comb over the stove.

As Eloise installed the extensions in my transitioning nappy hair, I got an experience I'll never forget.

"So now that you didn't get into nursing school, what's your plan?" she asked me with a smirk. I couldn't figure out what was funny to her, so I looked back at her with confidence and told her I was waiting on my acceptance letter at another attempt to get into nursing school.

Before I could say anything else, the room stopped, the voice from the television went mute, and my sister's question made me angry.

"Can you tell me why you keep applying to nursing school?" she asked me with irritation in her voice.

It was like she'd been waiting for this conversation. Before I could say anything, she told me how she felt about my desire to be a nurse.

"Amber, you're not going to get accepted into any nursing school," she said, looking like she had before hitting me upside the head in the park. I had so much to say to her, but I didn't know how to say it. I was furious with her.

It was one thing to be denied by an institution, but it was another to have your flesh and blood look at you and confirm its decision. Although my sister was wiser than me, heard from God too, and knew what I was capable of, her words hurt me to my core. It seemed like she didn't support my dreams.

REJECTION

I sat there with my face down and my hands needing a dry towel from the sweat that dripped onto my pants.

"Why would you say that?" I asked with great sadness. What she said next rocked me to my core.

"You're trying to walk in Ashley's calling. If you were to become a nurse, it would limit your ability to go to the places God is calling you to walk in. God made your feet to travel in places that not many will go. I know you want to be a nurse, but I wouldn't be your sister if I didn't tell you the truth. Your calling isn't to kill you literally, and until you realize that, you'll forever pay the price for a calling you can't afford."

I sat in that chair, quiet as a mouse. I wanted to respond, but I didn't know how to.

I sunk in the chair and cried.

Ashley graduated from the Capstone College of Nursing and was well on her way to furthering her nursing career. She made it look easy, and if it was easy, it was easy for her because it was her calling, not mine. I couldn't see what Eloise could see because I was vulnerable. I felt attacked and offended, too, even though I knew she supported me. No one pressured me to be like Ashley. I put pressure on myself to pursue a field that suited me and would make me a lot of money. I thought only nursing could provide that.

Eloise's words made sense, but it wasn't apparent to me because I hadn't yet accepted the path which would lead me to *my* calling - to empower women through healing relationships and inspire them to reach back and help someone else.

My plans weren't God's plans. I wanted to go in one direction, but God pulled me in another. When I let go and understood this, I grasped who I was: someone called, has a purpose, and is still loved regardless of the doors that weren't opening. I had to learn to accept who God was calling me to be, even if it didn't look the way I expected.

My dream to attend nursing school continued to die when I opened another denial letter from UA's nursing school. But I was still committed to my plan, so I wondered if I should even be at UA. I decided to apply to nursing school at another institution and got denied from that program. I found it funny that even after knowing that being a nurse wasn't for me, I was willing to give up being at UA to chase another school, a place God didn't even tell me to go.

I needed security about my future, security that eluded me.

Before returning to school, I visited my primary doctor and told him I couldn't focus. He prescribed Adderall, something I thought would fix the problem but couldn't. Focusing was not the problem, so Adderall didn't do me any good.

The tension to achieve gave me headaches, which turned into migraines. I was two years out from graduating with my bachelor's degree, and I had no plan. My lost sense of purpose drove me to question who I was, picking up the alcohol I swore I'd never drink again, treating people so coldly, and returning to places I vowed I'd never return to.

Not knowing my next step pushed me into insecurity. I needed to feel secure. Thinking I could find the security I was looking for in the arms of a relationship, I ran into a relationship with my arms wide open, and I didn't look back.

5

Sabbatical

I MET SAIRE DURING MY SOPHOMORE YEAR of college while doing my resident advisor floor rounds one night. He was an inch or two taller than me with a lean build. He was well-dressed with chocolate-brown skin to match his swagger. His floor was the last floor I completed my rounds on. Doing floor rounds was crucial to the job, so I tried to get them over with because I dreaded them.

As I cut the corner, Saire was coming out of a room I assumed was his.

"Hey there, how are you?" he asked me. I don't know what it was, but when he said hey to me, I could see the passion for people behind his smile, which was odd because

I didn't know him. After I said hey to him, he ran down the hallway to another room.

We didn't say too much that night because he was a resident. He wasn't my resident, which technically meant I didn't have to know him. Our first encounter was our last, until a few months later, when he attended an event a few girls and I hosted in my residence hall.

Saire had a way with people. He inspired young men to dive deeper into God, and he had excellent knowledge of the Word. The small group quickly snagged him to be our guest speaker for our back-to-school shindig.

He spoke with experience and shared pieces of his story with those who attended. He shared with the attendees about his platform. And he told of his dreams and aspirations, which sparked many to dive deeper into their dreams. After the event was over, I stayed to get to know some attendees and said hello to the organization leaders who supported the event. Saire stayed afterward to help us clean up; he wouldn't have been Saire if he'd not done so.

The community room emptied, and the automatic lights went dim. I sat down on a brown one-seat couch, and Saire sat on the couch beside me. I was giddy inside. I was intrigued after hearing him speak. But I didn't have any expectations because I was still healing and dealing with my own stuff. I was in the process of trying to put my worth in the right place: God alone.

"So what did you think about the event?" he asked me, smiling like he did when I saw him in the hallway the first time.

SABBATICAL

"It was nice. We were happy to have you speak because you're so relatable," I replied. "Well, thank you," he said. I told him he was welcome, then he asked me about my passions. Considering our paths had crossed briefly before this event, this encounter was thought-provoking to me. I told him what I was passionate about and let the conversation go on as long as possible.

I don't remember how we drifted off into the vulnerable end of the conversation, but I knew we'd gone far when I told him some of the most sacred pieces of me. It wasn't long before my finger went twirling my newly curled extensions, the extensions I used to cover up how I viewed my hair. I straightened up in that chair, pulled my lime green dress down below my knees, and the conversation between Saire and I got serious.

It was a Thursday night when he took me on our first date to a dope jazz spot in Tuscaloosa. It was a hole-in-the-wall spot, popular with an older diverse crowd. I hadn't told him I loved melodic jazz music, so his creativity and attention to my liking stood out to me.

The melodies fluidly playing from the live band could be heard outside as we got closer to the door. They reminded me of John Coltrane with a mix of Robert Glasper and Euge Groove. It was a feel-good vibe infused with R&B, and those sounds always struck me deep. The intimacy in the building comforted me before his hands could.

When we got to our table, Saire pulled out my chair. I noticed Sophia and one of Saire's friends were with us as I sat down. I was surprised because our first date came with accountability in the presence of two additional people.

HUPOMONE

This date with Saire set a standard for what I envisioned in the future. I smiled from ear to ear. I was the happiest girl.

The lights went dim, and Saire and I got close. For some reason, I thought about how Dejuan scooted his cot next to mine at nap time. Before I could make any assumptions about what Saire wanted from me, he told me he intended to honor God, then me. So I eased up and allowed myself to get close to him.

As we talked, Saire's friend and Sophia glanced over at us as if they were observing us. I tried not to think too deeply about what they were doing because when I overanalyzed, I created thoughts that weren't true.

I took a sip of water and told myself to take a chill pill.

I enjoyed that night with Saire like there was no tomorrow. We talked about what we wanted to do together and separately on campus. We both wanted to use whatever we'd become to bring people closer to God. Our first date, drenched in good intentions and accountability, left me overwhelmed with happiness. I went to sleep thanking God that maybe, just maybe, I could trust Saire with my heart.

After a few months, the good intentions from our first date had no follow-through, and things between us went downhill.

From the start, our relationship required accountability from outsiders. I didn't think this was problematic until I noticed that we were dysfunctional when it was just the two of us, with no middle man. The accountability wasn't there when we needed accountability.

Saire had a thing going with another girl, but our potential together and the hope for meeting our shared goals made me stay. I'd mistaken forgiveness for "forgive and let back in."

He wouldn't return my calls or texts when we argued, and I wondered where he'd gone. I thought about how Daddy would leave, and I never knew if or when he was coming back home.

When the rubber met the road, the truth was we weren't good together. I made a mental note that just because something looked good didn't mean it was good.

The average girl's dream is to be loved by her daddy. She watches how her daddy loves her mom because how her daddy loves her mom is how she believes she should be loved.

Daddy did a good job of loving me. However, his example of loving Momma led me to believe that being lied to and cheated on, amongst other things, were acceptable relationship standards for me. It led me to think that it was okay for a man to get it somewhere else when he couldn't get it from me. But at some point, I had to take some responsibility for myself.

Whether I like to admit it or not, the relationship was over when it began because anything that starts on a broken foundation is bound to crumble if not intentionally nurtured. I couldn't understand why I held on and chose to go on that trip to Tennessee with Saire anyways.

After a weekend of Tennessee mountain views, eating good food, watching black bears casually walk in the streets, getting pricked by tree limbs while hiking, and arguing here and there, the trip to Tennessee ended.

HUPOMONE

We stopped at Zaxby's for a quick bite to eat on our way back to Alabama. As we sat in the drive-through line, we listened to a podcast discussing Jonah and the fish.

The speaker went on and on about things I'd already learned about Jonah being in the fish. But the story took a turn when the speaker asked, "Is there someone in your boat weighing you down and distracting you from who God has called you to be?"

I got hot, my appetite left me, and I had to use the bathroom. I sat in the passenger seat wondering if he felt anything I was feeling, but I didn't ask.

Before I could fully process this question, Saire looked at me, appearing concerned, and said, "Amber, do you feel like I'm weighing your boat down?"

Immediately I thought about the waterfall we watched fall from the cliff that weekend. That was my second time seeing a waterfall in person, and all I could think about was being with Daddy on two waterfall occasions.

Daddy told me when I was too young to remember; he took Eloise, Ashley, and me to Noccalula Falls to watch the waterfall. I remember singing "don't go chasing waterfalls" with Daddy in his truck again. The message in that song hit me differently. And I couldn't help but wonder why I decided to go on that trip to save a relationship that I wasn't supposed to be in.

I choked on the dryness that clogged my throat because everything in me knew the answer to his question. My lips wouldn't move to say what we both knew.

"What made you ask me that question?" I asked him, super nervous to hear his answer.

"It's just a question I want to know the answer to," he said, trying to hide how he felt about it and how it *was* talking about our relationship. Everything in me wanted us, but I knew that we'd no longer be together when we got back to campus that evening.

I was right.

A couple of weeks later, I built up the courage to call Daddy and tell him that Saire and I ended our relationship.

"Heyyyyyy baby, how you doing?" Daddy answered, so happy and loud like he always answered the phone.

"Daddy, Saire and I broke up," I said, with hurt in my voice. The last time I was this messed up over a relationship was when Kree, my first love, left me.

"I knew that young man wasn't yours when I first met him," Daddy said, saying he told Momma the same.

"You knew this, Daddy, and you didn't tell me?" I asked. My face turned hot. I was angry with Daddy.

Why didn't he save me the trouble of having my heart broken? If Daddy told me what he thought at the beginning, could I have been saved from heartache? I wondered.

"Baby, I knew that man because I've been that man," he said. "I didn't tell you because you wouldn't have learned what you needed to learn about yourself and relationships if I'd told you. Besides, you've endured since you were born. I knew you'd get it. God is in you."

"I understand what you're saying, Daddy, but that's not fair, and my heart is now broken," I told him.

He apologized for my broken heart, but he didn't apologize for withholding information from me. He insisted he knew I'd get it.

HUPOMONE

While I feared losing someone I cared about, I learned I was more afraid of not dating anyone after a break-up. I didn't want to be alone. But I needed time and space to become myself. I needed to figure it out.

I couldn't be mad at Daddy like I wanted because in telling me the truth, he showed me that I'd found my worth by being in a relationship, too. I hung up the phone and let out a silent laugh because I knew it was time for me to face myself.

The dating culture told me that I needed to get in a relationship with someone else to get over someone. Still, it never conveyed that brokenness and hurt would carry into my new relationship if not dealt with from the root.

I learned that my desire to have a relationship put me on a path of hurt, which showed up in other areas of my life. For instance, how I treated people when a relationship hurt me. I was a mess, and it was no secret that I needed healing.

Placing my worth in love and success led to hopelessness. I needed to learn who Amber was, alone. No matter how scared I was to know myself, I had to let go of the fear holding me back. I knew that God could do more for me in a year of no dating than I could on my own. After all, my worth and identity comes from within, and Him, alone.

Saire left me with the very thing Dejuan came for, and Ali almost took, and for that, I had nothing but respect for him. After all, maybe, all boys didn't want one thing.

SABBATICAL

I faced my fear and committed myself to a year of no dating. I knew that if I allowed myself to go on this journey, I'd learn what I needed to become the woman I was supposed to be.

I had a skewed idea of what this journey would look like when I committed myself to a year of no dating. I thought it'd be rainbows and sunshine. Thoughts that I wouldn't feel lonely at night and my desire to have a relationship would quickly disappear. Ideas that I wouldn't struggle with my insecurities. However, in the beginning, everything I struggled with in relationships intensified when I wasn't in one.

There wasn't an instruction manual to lead me on this journey. I thought I was crazy for even going through with it. But I learned that to become myself, I would have to un-become myself.

I would start with letting go of everything I thought I was, and it'd be hard.

IN THE SUMMER, DURING THE WEEK, I was an operations assistant for housing in Tuscaloosa and a team leader at Whataburger back at home on the weekends. Sure, I was working hard. But I didn't realize that I'd, too, made myself busy to avoid facing what hurt me.

I can't tell you how many pounds I lost and gained again because of my frequent visits to Jim 'N Nick's BBQ. When I pulled up to order, they told me to drive ahead and often gave me a half-dozen free cheese biscuits. This behavior became a problem.

I spent most of my time in the corners of Heritage House Coffee, a local coffee shop in Tuscaloosa. Coffee shops were my go-to because they gave me solitude.

I arrived thirty minutes before they opened to get the table or the room everyone wanted. The room was always quiet and away from everyone. Baked oatmeal, a cup of coffee, a pen, and a journal became my best friends. They kept me going amid the healing.

On the lines of each page in my journal, I wrote what I was experiencing. I couldn't understand what was happening to me. I struggled to get a handle on my emotions and felt crazy when my feelings unloaded on me at once. It would've been easier to get in another relationship. However, the conviction I felt about being alone wouldn't leave me. I had no idea that saying yes to being single for a year would set me on a path that took all my energy, willpower, and perseverance. This journey wasn't what I bargained for, I still had no career plan, and I was a hot mess.

When cheese biscuits weren't comforting me in an unhealthy way, or me over-committing myself to an activity other than facing myself, I stayed at Sophia's apartment. I spent most weeknights on her couch, laying in my tears.

Sophia made it easy for me to let out my emotions while finding my footing. She loved me in truth, even when I didn't want to hear it. So before I began what was supposed to be my senior year of college, she dried my tears and told me to get up.

SABBATICAL

"Amber, it's time for you to get up and begin acting on what you keep begging God to do for you," she said, standing over me, handing me Kleenex and a plate of Italian smothered chicken with jasmine rice and green beans.

"I'm doing my best," I said.

"I also think it's time for you to reconsider leading small groups, deal with your hurt, and let someone else lead you," she said. Her voice faded as she stepped back into the kitchen. There was no room for me to say anything or ask questions because she'd seen how what I was doing wasn't working - wallowing in my sorrow.

No dating was lonely. It was one of the longest seasons I'd endured, and I learned many things about myself. Placing my worth in what I thought brought me value - love, food, and success - led me down a road of unhealthy patterns. At the root of these patterns was how I viewed purity.

My experience with Dejuan and Ali exposed me to love's physical and intimate side. When loneliness knocked on my door, I bit the bait of temptation and watched images that would never make me feel better. In other forms, temptation also came to me, like relationships, food, and alcohol. I tried to fill the voids, but loneliness and never-ending sadness crept in. Somehow I was still empty.

I'd gotten fed up with failing, so I let the light shine on every hurting area of my life by first admitting, again, that I wasn't okay.

How many people I abstained from meant nothing if what went on in my heart was corrupt. I had to ask myself what I was thinking about, listening to, and watching – all things that spoke into every move I made. It was up to me to fight back. So I started fighting, and I sat in the loneliness with a new perspective.

My unfulfilled yearning for love was due to missing God in my life. So I went to my closet and pulled out my journals to talk with God.

I stopped writing that summer because I didn't like the person I saw on those pages, but I realized that was the person I needed to see. I needed to know the pattern of falling for false love and making hasty decisions. I chose to stop running from this process and allowed myself to take my time.

I wrote in my mint green journal and prepared for my next year of college.

A FEW WEEKS AFTER THE SEMESTER BEGAN, I realized I'd chosen to reach for the "American Dream" when I was a little girl because I could give Momma the house she always wanted. My dream made me believe that my worth and value came from how much money I could make. Money was my metric for success.

Nursing offered me a financial peace that I didn't believe could come from anywhere else. I didn't have old money to support me while I figured out what I wanted to do with my life. Remaining single for a year forced me to rediscover who I was, what I liked, what I wanted out of life outside of money, and ultimately, what was God's will for my life.

SABBATICAL

I was still paying for a path God never called me to, which drained me. I practically lived in a one-person study room at Rodgers Library, drinking unhealthy amounts of coffee and energy drinks.

Sleep deprivation caused unnecessary stress, which made it hard to focus. I was sabotaging who I was for a life God didn't call me to live. God created me with gifts, passions, and talents, but I needed to learn to surrender my plans to live out the journey He handcrafted for me.

In the meantime, I began looking for other opportunities to grow. I planned my studies to go with what I liked, and I picked up a minor in communication studies.

Communication studies involved everything I was afraid of: connecting with others in groups again, public speaking, and understanding the importance of leading groups well. All three areas were a problem because I had no desire to be around people, I was an independent worker, and I didn't want a microphone or stage. The only thing that intrigued me about this path was my ability to work on my writing skills and learn about other cultures, even though I didn't know if I'd ever experience different cultures abroad.

I'd gotten desperate for God's will for me, so I turned off my phone and blocked all the distractions on a Friday night.

The smell of a mahogany teakwood candle filled my room. Contemporary jazz bounced off my walls. I whispered a small prayer and began writing in my journal.

I put all my effort into identifying what I did and liked as a little girl. I watched everything come to life on paper.

Music gave me peace, and dancing set me free. Nature allowed me to explore, and writing brought me joy and peace. I loved reading books and learning from them. I understood discipline, and I loved to plan. I could juggle multiple things simultaneously, and I didn't mind getting my hands dirty. I was a natural helper, challenger, and loyal to the work. Eloise was right: what I possessed couldn't be confined to a specific space.

A couple of months later, I got the courage to email a career advisor. After getting to know me, she guided me through taking the Strong Interest Inventory ® test. I scored the highest in spirituality, counseling, and healthcare. The test suggested three ideal career paths: speech pathology, nursing, and social work. After all the work I put in, the test told me nursing was suitable for me. I laughed out loud, literally.

I no longer wanted to pursue a career for financial comfort, but I also didn't want to choose a major that wouldn't compensate me for the debt I accumulated over the years – such a contradiction. Regardless, things were working, and I had to hold on until it all made sense.

Things began making sense when I found myself baking Christmas cookies that December with Sophia.

"There's the Christmas tree, and the ornaments are in the box in the corner," she yelled from the kitchen, preparing me yet another meal. Christmas time always made me happy, and I needed something to keep my mind off my reality of not knowing what was next. I put the tree up with ease, placing every limb nicely.

We were listening to Mariah Carey's "O Holy Night" when Sophia walked over to me from the kitchen and grabbed an ornament from my hand.

"Why did you take that from me like that?" I asked her, bothered.

"Look at me," she said, looking like Momma did with her strict facial gestures. For a second, the joy of Christmas left the room.

"What have I done now?" I asked her, rolling my eyes.

"Have you decided what you want your major to be?" she asked me, laughing as if she already knew.

Between Eloise telling me nursing wasn't it and Sophia asking me to look into what was for me, I was over this whole career thing. Nevertheless, by the end of that night, I changed my major to social work, a decision I had no idea was going to make over my life again.

———

I STOOD IN THE MIDDLE OF THE QUAD IN FEBRUARY. Cars, loud music, buildings, conversations, and nature surrounded me, along with a choice to do something different for myself.

A group of girls conversed about what they were wearing to a party that night. A dog leaped in the air for a Frisbee. A group of fashion students had taken over the nearby steps with their photo-shoot, and people studied under the big trees.

In the middle of it all, there I was too paralyzed to walk forward.

Anxiety painted the door that should've represented purpose for me. The last time I sweated through my clothes, I had to talk to a counselor about why I tried to commit suicide. There I was sweating again, making another big life decision. I didn't even know I was in a hole of failure because "what ifs" had crept in and left me there.

The campus bell tower rang.

Life was moving on, so I walked through the door.

"Have a seat right here, and someone will be with you in a few minutes," the student ambassador said.

I realized that it wasn't just the security of a high-paying job that I was running to. I was running from the reality of how changing majors would change how I viewed the world.

"Amber, you can come into my office now," the social work advisor told me, wearing a more prominent smile than mine.

I got up and followed her into her freezing-cold office. I was always freezing cold.

"So what brings you here today?" she asked me, tapping her pen on her crimson red and white notepad.

"I applied for nursing school three times and haven't gotten in. I'm tired of being denied. I want to do what's right for me," I said. She gave me a thought-provoking look, and I couldn't help but wonder if she was judging me.

"What is your campus-wide identification number (CWID)? I want us to look at your transcript," she said, clearly hoping I'd leave her office with a plan.

I gave her my CWID, and she clicked on my profile.

After telling me about social work, she looked at my grades and said I qualified for a few scholarships because my grade point average was high.

"I also see that you are graduating late. So if you need assistance to cover additional semesters, we have a financial assistance scholarship you can apply for," she said, speaking as if someone close to me had already told her of my situation.

Every class I'd previously taken transferred over, and I was now a social work major.

My old friend from back at the church that day was right; God wasn't honoring *my* plan because it wasn't *His* will for my life.

I let out a daring sigh because I was relieved that maybe, just maybe, things were coming together.

It was changing my major that brought highs and lows. The change brought my old wounds of feeling inadequate, because of where I came from, back to the surface. And healing took place all over again.

My past forced me to see myself on the side of the one society deems "lesser than." I felt challenged to have conversations about topics that once made me uncomfortable. The program taught me to hold steadfast to integrity while strengthening my ability to stand in front of people who disagree with me. I also met one of my best friends, Caitlin.

While my major change from nursing to social work unfolded beautifully, who I was as a writer was humbled.

"Today is the day you will take the writing exam," my professor said, dreading this exam as much as we were.

It was a timed exam, and students who failed had one more chance to take it. Students failing the exam the second time had to retake the entire class the following semester. I failed twice, setting back my graduation date again.. Everything in me tried finding the good in failure, but I couldn't. I was so tired.

I couldn't understand how a timed test could determine my ability to succeed at God's plan for my life. How a timed test could decide if I was a good writer or not. I discovered that I still had a long way to go, and the change to a social work major was doing a great job helping me remember that.

It was a late Friday night when I arrived back in Tuscaloosa from a small group. I took a seat at my desk and wrote until my hands were numb. Even amid failure, though it didn't feel like it, things worked together for my good. I saw the fruits of my *yes* to this journey, which I allowed myself to go on.

I was good and rested peacefully in the quietness of the night.

Despite all the goodness, I woke up in pain in the middle of the night. My body felt like it was on fire, and moisture soaked my bed sheets. I was weak, and the pain in my stomach was debilitating. The stabbing pain made it difficult for me to get up and walk. As I continued to try and get up, I fell out of my bed. I rallied all the strength in my frail body and crawled to the bathroom, where I threw up everything I'd eaten that week (or so it seemed). All I could think about was being a baby again, wondering whether life or death existed on the other side of my pain. Something brewed inside me. I knew it was there, but I didn't know what it was.

The hospital admitted me, and the doctor said I was pregnant.

6

Pregnant

After selling my Kia Sephia the previous summer, my uncle bought me a 2006 Red Toyota® Camry. Having a new car was such a gift because I could drive to Auburn for a small group every Friday that semester. I was driving three hours to be in the community at the home of Mr. D and Mrs. M. They were preparing us to go on a mission trip to the Dominican Republic. Although I had a car, my friend Tasha allowed me to alternate between my car and her SUV to save miles on my vehicle.

I met Tasha in 2013. Together, we were resident advisors in our residence hall. She reminded me of Beyoncé with her many talents. Her ability to play and understand music was impeccable, her heart for philanthropic work was inspiring, and her unmatched work ethic challenged me. Her contagious personality changed the dynamic of any room she walked in. She didn't believe in excuses, and if you told her your wildest dreams, she checked in on you to ensure you were achieving your goals to make that dream happen. Her heart for people being true to themselves led me to open up to her about my flaws.

The first few people to see where I come from were Jamese and Tasha. I didn't show many people where I come from because I thought people would judge me for it. With Tasha, I didn't need to wear a mask, and it felt good.

When Porcia died, I stopped laughing, and Tasha helped me reconnect with my comical side. My resting face always stood in the way of my smile. Like so many others, she eased me into taking ownership of my story. She believed in who I was more than she believed in who I'd become. She entrusted me with her car so I could find freedom through the small group and fulfill another level of my purpose.

I don't know if excitement had gotten in the way, but I couldn't understand how I signed up to go on a mission trip with a group of students three hours away.

We met every Friday leading up to our mission trip to the Dominican Republic. I was the only black student in our group of twenty, and for a moment, I wondered if they viewed me like those four white guys that night they called me a nigger. They didn't.

PREGNANT

On Fridays, we held each other accountable, got our assignments for the trip, occasionally toasted marshmallows, chocolate, and graham crackers over a fire, and drank coffee. Everything about those Fridays was so good.

Three hour drive there. Two hours for the meeting. Three hour drive back. There were pieces of me I hadn't yet accepted about myself, or dealt with, that being alone on those drives showed me. Those rides revealed to me that hurt and pain was still hidden in my heart, and I needed to let them go.

While still learning how to let go of what was hurting me internally, I physically got sick and was put in the hospital.

After being admitted to the hospital, Momma and my friends rushed to the hospital to check on me. They prayed for me, brought me flowers, and made me smile. My cell phone wouldn't stop ringing. Momma was happy to see that I had a community of friends while away from home, but I knew she wanted to know if I was okay.

"Has anyone told you what's wrong?" Momma asked me, concerned. Even though I knew I wasn't pregnant, I couldn't tell Momma they thought I was pregnant, so I just told her I hadn't heard anything.

My thoughts were all over the place.

Pregnant. How? How was I pregnant? I knew how a woman gets pregnant, but I couldn't understand how I was pregnant. I had my fair share of testing the waters, but I'd never gone *far enough* to get pregnant.

I laid in the hospital for a few days, where my body was a pincushion for testing, and medical staff pricked my flesh more than I could count. I saw my doctor once and got word he wouldn't return until later that week. So I stayed, waiting for him to come back.

I didn't want to look in my doctor's eyes and tell him he was wrong, but everything in me knew he was. I knew I wasn't pregnant.

At the end of that week, he returned with an overload of confidence about my diagnosis.

"How are you feeling, Amber?" he asked me, standing tall with fair skin and quite attractive.

"I'm okay," I said. "I just hate that I'm missing class and hope I can still go on my mission trip," I informed him.

"Well, Amber, do you mind if everyone leaves the room for a few minutes?" he said, looking puzzled. That concerned me.

Everyone left the room, and Momma stayed with me.

He rolled his chair over to my bedside, and his soft hands touched mine.

"I want to do what makes you comfortable," he said, his wintergreen breath sweeping over my face. "Would you like your mom to leave?"

"It's okay if she stays," I told him, because whatever he had to say to me, she needed to know, and at this rate, she wasn't going to leave the room anyway.

"Amber, you're presenting symptoms of a pregnant woman," he told me again while looking at Momma out of the corner of his eyes like he was scared of her.

Momma's head took the slowest turn in my direction, and her eyes began telling me everything she was thinking.

PREGNANT

"I'm not pregnant," I told him with confidence. I needed Momma to stop staring at me, so I told him to run a pregnancy test.

"Before I run the test, are you sure there isn't a chance you're pregnant?" he asked me again. I wanted to throw the cup of ice next to me because he was irritating me, and I knew I wasn't pregnant.

"Yes, I'm sure," I told him.

An hour had gone by when he returned with a negative pregnancy test. The lab reports detailed what was going on with my body.

An infection in my body caused my lymphocyte blood cells to decrease, leaving me with almost none. He stated that the normal red blood cell count in a woman was thirty-six to forty-eight, and because my level was twenty-six, I was anemic, which explains why I was cold, throwing up, bleeding, and dehydrated.

The word "pregnant" had been put into my mind so much that week that I started wondering with what. I suppose I was bearing pain close to a pregnant woman, but I wasn't carrying a child's life. I was nurturing something spiritual that went beyond what my human mind could understand, and this doctor's initial thoughts proved it. The impact of this sickness, right as I was about to leave for the Dominican Republic, showed me that God was still at work within me. He went to great lengths to sit me down, and I had no choice but to listen to Him.

A few days later, I was discharged from the hospital and went to stay with my college faculty advisor. She was a wise woman and intentional in her relationships. Her house was a safe haven for young women, and she made sure I slept until the rest recharged my body for the weeks ahead.

My health improved, Spring Break 2015 arrived, and I left for the Dominican Republic.

When I tucked my new passport in my purse, grabbed my suitcase, and loaded up my Camry, it was approaching midnight. I was making my last three-hour drive to Auburn. A lot happened behind me, so I anticipated everything in front of me.

I pulled up to the Waffle House, where my group and I devoured waffles and hash browns, and drank several cups of coffee. Then we drove to our meeting spot, loaded our belongings into the van, and drove to Atlanta, Georgia. That drive was long and tedious in the van, so I pulled out my neck pillow and went to sleep.

When I woke up, we were at the Hartsfield-Jackson Atlanta International Airport, a place I'd never been, making this my first time flying on a plane.

The flashing lights from the planes lit up like stars in the sky. The airport was huge with a lot of traffic. People were in a hurry, and I moved out of their way so I wouldn't get knocked down. Carts of suitcases and continuous activity were everywhere. The people who checked us in spoke with authority and demanded we cooperate.

The ticket agent signaled that I'd come to the desk. I gave her my driver's license and passport. I put my

PREGNANT

overloaded suitcase on the scale and stepped back to make sure it weighed under fifty pounds, and it did.

The ticket agent told me that my Clinique facial cleansers were over the liquid limit. Because my suitcase had already slid its way through the conveyor belt, I had a choice: I could trash the cleansers or pay over one hundred dollars to carry them on. I paid the money and carried them on. I don't know what I was thinking.

Carrying two bags, I lunged my way up to security, and an uneasy feeling fell over me. I took my heels off, placed my belongings in the gray bins, and stepped up to be inspected by security. I was told to step out, examined again, and set free to go on the other side of the gates. I threw my bags over my shoulders and bent down to strap my heels around my ankles.

I stood up and made my way toward my group. The closer I got to them, the more I felt one of my heels wobble. I began losing my balance and tried to catch myself. I lost my balance and fell in the middle of the airport.

I sat in the middle of the floor with my head down and my body shaking.

I was embarrassed.

Being on the airport floor reminded me of when I tripped over my heels, wearing my bed-sheet wedding dress when I was a little girl.

Why did I wear heels to the airport in the first place? I was carrying so much baggage and didn't pack light. I didn't know how to. My internal and external bags had gotten in the way, and I was left limping through the airport until I got my other shoes out of my carry-on.

I loved how those heels made me feel. They gave me comfort. They were my identity. I didn't want to take them off because I knew I'd have to face the reality of who I was if I took them off.

I was holding a broken heel and carrying the weight of humiliation.

Checkpoint agents cleared my group to board the plane. As I held back every tear, I walked through the jetway to get on my flight.

One of the guys from my small group offered me his window seat, insisting I needed to see what life above the clouds looked like since it was my first time flying. His thoughtful gesture gave me some hope.

I stashed my belongings above my head, sat down in my window seat, buried the side of my face in the window, and I cried.

The flight attendant was going on and on about flight safety. But I checked out after she told us to secure our masks first before helping anyone else in an emergency.

As the plane ascended toward the heavens, who I wasn't within was descending. It was time to stop playing it safe and let go of everything that had me bound.

That afternoon we landed in the Dominican Republic to palm trees and clear blue skies.

A group of Dominican men in colorful suits and straw hats said hello to us.

PREGNANT

"Bienvenida a Republica Dominicana morena," one man said to me, smiling and playing his guitar. I didn't know what "morena" meant, but I smiled back at him, received his welcome, and jigged a little bit with him anyways.

Being there blew me away because these were things I'd seen on television, never in person. I never thought I'd see these things in person.

After we made it through security, a Dominican man with a bald head, wearing a white t-shirt, black flip-flops, and blue jeans, slid his way through the herd of people and introduced himself as our guide for the week. He loaded our belongings in the vans and drove us to our home.

My head hit the ceiling every time we drove over the potholes. The city we were in looked like a mixture of poverty and beauty. The air smelled horrible, and my stomach was in knots. Men on motorcycles with women sitting on the back, holding their babies, flew past our van. Little boys and little girls were bathing outside in broad daylight, and women walked by, balancing baskets of fruit on their heads. At the traffic lights, young boys cleaned windows, and people gave them money. This culture was different.This world was new and there was so much for me to take in.

Late that evening, we arrived at the house, located on the outskirts of the communities we'd serve. It was in a dead-end location at the end of a silent street. The ocean and a closed water park sandwiched the house.

Before making our way in, we stood outside the gates and received the rules of the house. We then found our rooms and unpacked our bags. We had a few minutes to get situated before we were to report to the patio in the backyard for a team meeting.

I know Mr. D. explained a lot to us, but I checked out when he told me that I'd be giving my testimony in the villages the following day. Fear and anxiety were dancing at my door, and after this news, I let them in.

In my head, I was unqualified to speak because of my brokenness – the pain from my unhealthy relationships, where I come from, dealing with a broken heart, and still trying to understand God's plan for my life.

I had a lot of growing to do within myself. That's why I didn't want to speak about my story. I could certainly talk to a group, but I hadn't grasped the gift of empowering people with my story. Because, after all, it wasn't about me.

It was up to me to take advantage of all the ways God blessed me. While Mr. D. called me to share my story, I knew it was God that would give me the strength to do it. So that evening I gathered my belongings, settled in my room, pushed my broken heels aside, and went to bed.

At half-after five the next morning, the roosters woke me up. Today was the day, and whether I was ready or not, I'd be sharing my testimony.

I stole a moment to myself in the shower outside. I rehearsed my testimony over and over until I memorized it. When I felt confident, I made my way to the kitchen to help prepare breakfast for the team.

PREGNANT

"Amber, today is the day," Mr. D. said to me in passing, smiling big and proud. I gave him a stare with a subtle smirk because I was nervous.

Mr. D. and Mrs. M.'s commitment to their work was unwavering. They were parents of three children and worked full-time jobs while pouring into students' lives. They balanced it well, and it was inspiring.

Mrs. M. sat this trip out, but you better believe the entire group felt her prayers and presence. Mr. D. wasn't just our leader on the trip; he was like our dad. Integrity and character meant everything to him, and he challenged us to honor the task we'd carry out.

Mr. D. and Mrs. M. saw something in me – purpose - that I was *still* learning to see, so I shouldn't have been surprised when he asked me to share my testimony. But I was.

We loaded up the van, and I claimed another window seat in the back. After a long bumpy ride, we arrived in the village, and it was time for me to speak.

I stood under the shack in a daze. In shock over where I was, what I was seeing, and what was happening, I forgot the testimony I memorized and spoke from an authentic and vulnerable place. I talked about my rejection letters to nursing school, what dating had done to me, and how I was still learning to be me. After sharing my testimony, I played tag and threw the ball with the kiddos from the village.

After a few hours of serving and playing, we loaded up the van and returned home.

I was alone on the roof that evening, reflecting on the day. I wrote in my journal as tears drenched the pink shirt I wore. What I hadn't realized was that my memorized testimony was glossy. I wrote the sugar-coated pieces of my mess and left out the parts where God showed Himself faithful when I was a mess.

When I shared my story's intricate details and how God worked in my brokenness, it stopped a young mom considering suicide and a dad from leaving his family. God worked through my story to reach others, and I was humbled. It wasn't about me.

Standing in the middle of a place unknown, I allowed God's story of love and grace over my life to give hope to men and women on the other side of the world. God was stretching me, and much like Mr. D., He was making sure I grew and developed in the face of what was making me uncomfortable. Mr. D. commissioned me to give my testimony again the next day in the school, where I'd served two more times over the years.

The next morning, we arrived at the school to work with the kids who attended school there. I've always had a passion for kids, and they naturally gravitated toward me.

On this day, Mr. D challenged us to put our phones down and connect with where we were. That meant no pictures were to be taken. It was a challenge I didn't understand but a challenge I needed.

After observing everything around me, things became more apparent, and it was up to me to seek God before I could share Him with others. I no longer ran from the opportunity to grow. Instead, I ran toward the opportunity to be stretched. It took being in the moment to see that. Mr. D. was right after all.

PREGNANT

Before I left Tuscaloosa for Auburn, I lay in the middle of my floor and pleaded with God to help me understand what He was doing in my life. That week, He did. By the third day, I was unbecoming everything I thought I was and thought I wanted.

On the first day, when I gave my testimony in that village, we passed by the school where we played with the kids, and I noticed a group of little girls standing in the street. Something about these girls stirred my heart.

God told me to sponsor a little girl from the group for a year. Through sponsorship, I learned that the reality of how I viewed what life afforded me as a little girl -- the little I thought I had -- was nothing compared to what she is accustomed to -- the little she does have compared to mine.

After spending almost four days playing with the children in the school, God gave me four words: *degrees, foreign soil, books, and agencies*. I didn't know what those words meant but I wrote them down and put them to rest with me that night.

With two days left in the Dominican Republic, Mr. D told me I was to give the devotional to the team the following day, and I didn't want to. I was overwhelmed by the things that happened just days before -- my previous testimony, the little girls in the school, and the letting go of me -- and honestly, I didn't think I had the energy to pour out anything else. I did what he asked me, though.

I planned to share from Jeremiah 29:11, but nothing I rehearsed came out of my mouth the next morning.

The sky was dim, the roosters didn't crow, and the birds didn't sing that morning.

As I headed down to the patio to share what I'd prepared, God whispered a few words to me, "Amber, if you can't let me speak to you, then I can't let you speak to them."

I thought I was undone but I was nowhere near it.

I put together a devotional I wasn't yet ready to teach. I'd gotten so used to leading small groups that I forgot what it was like to be still and listen. By this point, I knew my group thought I was some emotional girl who cried all the time because I let go of every tear I held back and didn't care.

I shared more about who I was and what I'd been through for the first time. My obedience to throw away a devotional, not ready for me to share, inspired others to let go of their tears. The power at work in the room reshaped everyone in their unique ways. Our week in the Dominican Republic changed our lives for the better.

By the end of the week, I'd been invited back to the Dominican Republic to serve in the school the following October.

When we arrived at the airport, we learned there was a delay in our flight returning home. At first, I was unbothered, but that changed when I realized I was turning twenty-two the next day, and class started Monday morning.

We arrived at the Miami airport at one o'clock in the morning, and Mr. D. told us to get comfortable because we were staying the night there. We unpacked our bags and went to sleep on seaweed-green cots.

While everyone dozed off to sleep, I stopped because the last time I slept on a cot, Dejuan touched me underneath my covers, a memory that hadn't yet faded.

I was going home changed and understood that I still had a long way to go.

I WAS ON AN ODD HIGH WITH ALL the life-changing events happening in my life. I built stamina in the Dominican Republic, intending to use that stamina to sustain me when I got back to Tuscaloosa.

God moved significantly in my life that week, but the pain I held on to became more prominent than what God was doing in my life. I hadn't yet understood that healing takes time, and wholeness doesn't happen overnight. I tapped into a deeper revelation of my purpose on the other side of the world, but I crumbled the moment I got back home.

I went from sharing my testimony of God's faithfulness, in a foreign country, to still bearing the pain from my breakup with Saire and hurting others in the process.

I forgot all of God's plans for me.

7

Humbled

I RETURNED TO TUSCALOOSA, miserable. The places I went to on a typical day left me irritated. I was no longer ambitious about my classes. My role as a resident advisor was on the line because of my poor work performance. I had no desire to leave my dorm room, I didn't care to be around people, and I cut my phone off often.

My purpose -- to empower women through healing and relationships, and inspire them to reach back and help someone else -- was awakened. But, my character and integrity came into question when I hurt others because I was still holding on to the hurt and pain from my breakup. I struggled with who God revealed I'd become but wasn't yet.

HUPOMONE

"Amber, do you want others to know you love God more than you want God to know that you love Him?" Carmen asked me on the phone that night. I sat on my bedroom floor shell-shocked. The phone was silent because I didn't know what to say.

I met Carmen my freshman year, and I had no interest in being her friend. She wasn't a bad person. At the time, she appeared to be intense and it made me uncomfortable. She had an aura that yelled "no-nonsense." She didn't care about being on the scene, including social media. While she was sharp in her approach, I learned overtime that she was personable.

She was the type of person who gave you a mirror to look at yourself. She sharpened the inner me before the outer me stood before others. She helped me play into my strengths while not forgetting my weaknesses. Through our relationship, I understood the importance of sitting with my reasons for not liking something, which often meant I didn't understand it.

When she asked me that question, I had no choice but to check my intentions.

I'd done the ambitious, "college Christian girl" thing so well: I led small groups, prayed every morning, went on a mission trip, and interned with my local church in Tuscaloosa. I juggled my academics, jobs, and extracurricular activities exceptionally well. I inspired others, but when I forgot I was still human, I became a total joke in the eyes of many. The pain from healing from a relationship can do that to you if you let it - I let it.

Parties became my outlet. Skin-tight dresses hugged my Coke-bottle figure and became the foundation of

HUMBLED

my identity. If my character, speech, and way of life were someone's frame of reference in getting to know and following God, I missed the mark. Having great faith meant nothing if I didn't know how to use what I learned when standing face-to-face with the people who hurt me.

It didn't matter how many pictures I took with children in developing countries, I went back home, and my life picked up right where it left off.

After that conversation with Carmen, one of my other friends immediately called me and asked me another question that required me to sit with myself.

"Amber, take a moment and ask yourself where you got lost," Frida said to me most lovingly. I knew where I got lost, and she did too.

"We both know where. I just want this process to be over," I said, exhausted.

Frida was a member of my first small group who became a friend. She was one of the faithful few who stuck beside me when I wasn't myself. She wasn't afraid to get in the trenches with me because she knew the trenches would make me better. She was out to preserve the best of who I was and that began with getting honest with me.

Frida reminded me I wasn't ordinary. And if I was going to be a leader, I needed to know how to be led first. I found that alarming because those were the exact words Sophia told me the night we put up her Christmas tree.

A few days later, Frida and Sophia put together a surprise birthday party for me. I opened the door to Sophia's house, and the women there showered me in love. They didn't give up on me.

HUPOMONE

The anniversary of my "no dating for a year" came the next week, and I took myself out to dinner to reflect on everything that happened that year. I'd given myself the space to discover who I was apart from someone else.

I finally began to shake hands with healing.

Summer 2015 arrived, and the campus was quiet. Parking spots were plentiful, people were gone, and the flowers were blooming.

I had a routine. Monday through Friday I worked as an operations assistant, and at night I was a desk assistant. I left for Whataburger on Friday and returned to Tuscaloosa on Sunday. Then I did it all over again on Monday.

I spent some much-needed time with Porcia's mom on one Friday night that summer. We played with their dogs and watched Porcia's favorite movie series, *Twilight*. We made chocolate chip cookies, went through old pictures, and celebrated Porcia's life together. Since Porcia's death, this was our first time together, and we both needed it. We'd never talked about how much Porcia's death affected us. Her unexpected death had an odd way of keeping me quiet about how her death impacted me.

But on this night, all the words we needed to say, and hear, came out.

"I was going through Porcia's clothes and I want you to have this dress," Porcia's mom said, handing me the last dress I saw Porcia in two months before she died. I took the dress from her, trying to keep my emotions together.

Porcia's mom is resilient and so strong, so I did my best to hold back the tears. I had some difficult questions that I wanted to ask, but I couldn't bring myself to ask them, so I just followed her lead in the conversation.

As we spoke about her passing, we discussed how her passing changed the entire course of my life, for the better.

I couldn't hold back the tears any longer.

For the longest time, I misunderstood Porcia's death – a death that almost led me to my own. No matter how hard it was to believe that amid the tragedy Porcia's death brought, God was right there, watching and loving us through it all. We still had purpose despite her no longer being here with us. We just had to dig deep to find it. We had to find it, for our own life's sake.

Porcia lived a beautiful, abundant life, leaving a legacy beyond what I believe her womb would've ever produced. Her life was orchestrated, not just for her but also for those connected to her. And I'm still learning every day to rest on that promise.

Her sudden death gave us an unwanted end, but it gave me an answered prayer that forced me to run my race.

My final year at UA started unusually. I received a text message from my roommate from my sophomore year. It shocked me that day because this was the same girl who told me she didn't understand my faith in God.

I couldn't explain it to her at the time because I was still trying to figure it out, even in all my hiccups. But I knew God was real.

"Do you remember my freshman year, your sophomore year, when you kept asking me what was wrong with me because I stopped coming out of my room?" she texted me.

I had to take a moment to think about her question because that was the time I was healing from my suicide attempt.

"Yes, I remember. Was everything okay?" I replied. Her texts came in like a flood.

She met her then-boyfriend in college. After a month of dating, her boyfriend took her virginity and broke up with her. She spent her days waiting for him to call. The very depression that walked with me down that long hallway my freshman year became her best friend, locked up in the room with her, her freshman year.

She bolted herself and her pain on the other side of her bedroom door, seeing no way out. Her grades fell, and she failed some classes too. Every time she glanced in the mirror, a piece of glass cracked, leaving her with a skewed vision of herself. The clubs were her coping mechanism, as if partying was the only way she knew to make it "better." In less than two months, she lost twenty plus pounds.

I was my roommate, and my roommate was me.

She knew she was a good woman, but she couldn't see it at the time.

Suicide was a choice she almost made, but before it was, she packed her bags and left UA.

When she got home, she found herself sitting on the back row at church, where she let go of everything that had broken her. God was pulling her into a community of

HUMBLED

people, and she accepted it one night. It took her three years to understand why I was the way I was, and she couldn't do anything but thank me for being me and trusting in God.

Everything continued to come full circle by the summer's end, and I thanked God.

It was mid-October when I boarded my second plane back to the Dominican Republic. This time I flew alone. I was back to serve on a woman-only mission trip with a group of six women from Massachusetts. Yet again, I was the only black girl. I was also the youngest woman.

I soaked up so much from those women. Some were retired, married, and others were approaching their thirties, sharing much wisdom. I connected more profoundly with the children and families in the communities. I learned more about the culture and history of the organization I served with. I'd been given a second chance in the Dominican Republic to be better when I returned home.

I was leading and being refined more and more for my purpose. None of the doors that opened for me made sense because I already knew I needed to step back from leading, so this trip was baffling.

The trip ended with me contracting a respiratory infection and getting poison ivy.

The hospital treated me, and I came home to a letter from one of the older women who went on the trip with me.

While on the trip, she told me she'd send me a book she insisted I read: Dave Ramsey's *Total Money Makeover*. She told me she watched me sit back in silence as they spoke of money, and she wanted to pour into my financial knowledge.

God provided another person to invest in me, pushing me to be who He called me.

I LEARNED OVER TIME THAT RELATIONSHIPS, small groups, are necessary for human connection and growth. Small groups brought strangers together for a semester and turned strangers into friends. Small groups by design reminded me that community leads to relationships.

Sophia, Carmen, and Frida were right: I didn't need to lead anyone; I needed to be led. I didn't want to be why someone was in bondage, because I was. So I signed up for a Freedom Group with my local church in Tuscaloosa.

Freedom had an explicit curriculum with the singular purpose to lead individuals on a journey of liberation. While food and casual conversation made the community a great place, it wasn't the substance or foundation. The work we each *chose* to put in to get free is the basis of the positive impact of Freedom.

My small group was different. It was small in number, and God told the leader who to include in the small group. My leader was a woman who mentored me in an after-school program when I was a little girl, and a friend of Sophia and her friends assisted my leader in leading.

It was thirteen weeks of homework, demanding that we strip every negative belief we once had about ourselves in exchange for who God's word says we are. Thirteen weeks of discipline and perseverance. Thirteen weeks of unlearning it all for who God had already designed us to be. Thirteen weeks of sharing my feelings and hurts that I buried a long time ago, even after counseling.

Thirteen weeks abruptly led to a Thursday night where I dismantled the shame I wore and began snatching back my freedom.

In that intimate living room that night, I was covered from head to toe with shame and defeat. The lights were dim, the candles burned, and soft music bounced off the walls. I sat on the brown couch next to the front door. The room got thick with heat. My body started dripping sweat, and my chest grew tight. I was hesitant about being this vulnerable with them. But I knew it was time for me to get raw with my group, for myself. I didn't want to, but I did.

There was no shame or judgment in the room that night - we all could just be. Much of my shame, leading up to this night, resulted in me covering up the very things people could already see. But that all changed when the woman at the Freedom conference prayed over me.

A conference hosted for all the people who participated in a Freedom group closed out the thirteen weeks. It convened a day and a half at a convention complex.

On the first night, the speaker talked about how what someone is dealing with can often transfer into our spirits when entering relationships. That truth pierced our hearts because we knew it was true. When the speaker finished, some people stayed seated, some went up for prayer, and some returned to their rooms. I was desperate for prayer,

HUPOMONE

so I got up from my chair and stood at the end of the line, staring down the aisle.

I stepped up to the woman who would pray over me.

"What's your name?" she asked me, her smile comforting me before she prayed over me. "Amber," I said, realizing that was the first time I said my name out loud in a long time.

She just looked at me. I looked back at her, freaked out.

She stood there and kept staring at me. She grabbed my hand and hugged me. She placed my head on her shoulders, and she whispered, "The very thing you think disqualifies you is the very thing God wants to use to carry out His purpose for your life. It's your weakness that will connect you to people."

I stood there, and I balled.

How did this woman know I felt disqualified? How did this woman know I felt weak? How did this woman know my weaknesses had me feeling not good enough? I thought.

After she hugged me for what seemed like minutes, I got up and headed for our hotel room.

As I made my way to pay for my room, I felt this strong urge in my Spirit to drive back to Tuscaloosa instead. I was hesitant because it was December, it was freezing outside, and it was close to midnight.

I sat in my car contemplating what I should do, knowing that the drive back to Tuscaloosa would place me back in my dorm room at one o'clock in the morning.

The drive back wouldn't have been a problem if I hadn't had to be back at the conference the next morning by seven o'clock. It'd mean I'd have to get up at five o'clock in the morning to get ready and be back on time. I'd already packed nightclothes, so I bargained with God and thought to stay with a friend nearby. However, that door didn't open because she had a full house that night. My last resort was to drive to Momma's house, a few minutes away.

I crept up Momma's steps like I was in high school again, trying to make curfew, but she had locked the screen door. I wanted to wake her up to let me in, but she had no idea I was even in Birmingham. So, I drove back to Tuscaloosa.

While it didn't make sense, that morning I learned that God was protecting me from what I sought healing from, and He went to great lengths to do so, even if that meant I got four hours of sleep the night before.

God's protection for me helped everything connect. The rejections, the redirections, the process, the healing, the no dating, it was all divine.

Good things came from what seemed like never-ending sadness in my no dating for a year. Instead of seeking closure, I started seeking myself. I began learning how to extend myself grace and discovered that the longer I was in something, the longer it may take to get out, mentally and emotionally.

I understood that I must love myself first as far as relationships go. What someone brings to a relationship is an asset, but no one will complete me as God can. Seeking to fill my voids with a person can lead to codependency; God gently helped me anchor myself to Him alone.

I stopped managing my pain and started feeling my way through it. I wanted to learn how to forgive, not just those who hurt me but myself for the part I played in my hurt. I understood that I wouldn't become who God created me to be as long as I held on to everything I wasn't.

I'd gotten comfortable with where I was, and I was willing to give it another year.

I was becoming whole again.

8

Hupomone

It was a cold dewy morning in January 2016 when Momma texted Ashley and me and told us our grandfather, Momma's daddy, was in the hospital. She asked us to come home because he kept asking her where we were and if we were coming home.

I decided to go home that weekend, but he died before I could get there.

Celebrating granddaddy's life was calm for me because I had to speak at his funeral. I needed to keep it together for Momma and my aunt, so I did the best I could.

His death gave me valuable lessons. When the elders ask for your presence, they ask for a reason; listen to them and go. You must finalize earthly affairs, and if you can, leave something behind for your family - all the things he did.

It seemed like I'd shaken hands with death at the start of the New Year. Right after we buried Granddaddy, a few weeks later, Bradford passed away. To me, his death was sudden. All I heard ringing in my ears was him singing "Ordinary People," reminding me to take this life slowly.

The following summer, I went on a two-week study abroad trip to Mexico. I received a scholarship and financial assistance to study social services and Spanish. While I was there, death said hello again. My sister's best friend suddenly passed away. All those deaths reminded me that I don't always have the time I think I do.

When I returned from Mexico, I returned to my usual summer routine. I worked as an operations assistant and desk assistant in my residence hall in Tuscaloosa, and on the weekends, I commuted to Birmingham to work at Whataburger. By the summer's end, I was tired.

After five and a half years, my final semester at UA had finally come.

I worked my last freshman move-in, led my last first residence hall meeting, and participated in my last back-to-school WOW activities. My focus was on graduating. But of course, I had to experience some things before I could graduate.

I began the semester volunteering as an administrative assistant to an online premier lifestyle magazine while also doing my internship. While much of my work with the magazine challenged me to go deeper into the gifts and talents I possessed, the events that happened at my internship marked me.

To graduate, I had to complete a fifteen-week field practicum, with a minimum of four-hundred-fifty hours in an assigned agency. We were allowed to choose our top three agencies. I chose two medical settings and a student setting. I received an interview with *Student Care and Well-Being*, a department in the Dean of Students I was matched with.

I sat in a gray chair in the corner of the office, tapping my black heels on the gray and red carpet. I bit my nails down to the skin. I was sick of my heart racing every time an event made me nervous. As I attempted to get my nerves in check, the receptionists called my name.

"Amber Underwood, they are ready for you," she said, her hair styled in an Afro. She wasn't the lady from the counselor's office my freshman year, but she looked close enough.

"Okay, thank you," I said.

I sat in the chair for a minute because this room looked familiar.

I was back in the same office I came to *after* I finished counseling my freshman year of college. *What was going on*, I wondered. No wonder I was anxious.

As I made my way to the back, all I could think about was the documents in this office bearing my name. I was interviewing to be a social work student intern, and

I bombed the interview because I knew they knew who I was and what I tried.

I felt that hiring me, an attempted-suicidal individual, may not be a good look for them. I wanted to disqualify myself, and I almost did, but this time I held on to the hope that maybe that's not how they saw me.

I was right.

I became a social work student intern, advocating for students in crisis. Everything with my suicide attempt was coming full circle.

In my last semester of college, I had to go back to the beginning to identify what led me to my suicide attempt. As the memories seeped their way back into the parts of me that still needed healing, I went back to deal with them. It all started with a dark, muggy day in September, a day I'll never forget.

My day started like most of my other workdays. I stopped at Chick-fil-A to get some Chick-n-Minis and hash browns with a Coke and coffee, and made my way to the office.

"Good morning," I said to the receptionists. She smiled back at me like she always did and told me to remember to smile.

I sat down at my desk and did all things administration-related. I checked my emails and voicemails, transferred meal money to students, opened new cases, and closed old ones.

Around lunch, a chilling feeling came over me. Whenever I got this feeling, it meant something was about to happen or was happening. It's one of the ways God spoke to me.

I got the news a student had attempted suicide. The department asked me to go to the hospital with my supervisor to check on her.

As we walked down the hallways of that hospital, I realized I was standing in the hospital again, but this time it wasn't for me.

As I stared into the student's eyes, I started to see what I looked like in the eyes of my family and friends my freshman year, and it hurt. This student was in pain, and I knew that type of pain. I held back every tear I wanted to cry.

My instructions were to give her words of encouragement, let her know that resources were available to her, and share my story of overcoming wanting to die. I knew my experience wouldn't heal her, but it'd let her know she wasn't alone.

When we returned to the office, we received another complex case: my first case of human trafficking. These were too much for me in one day. And I couldn't understand why all this was happening simultaneously.

This student reminded me that often the ones we label "crazy" aren't crazy. Something happened for them to behave the way they do. This student's "normal" wasn't my "normal", and I needed to understand that.

After everything necessary was said and done, I darted across campus to return to my dorm room that evening.

I was relieved to be on the other side of that office door, and I had no intentions of replaying anything about that day. The degree of care expended in each case mentally and emotionally beat me.

I love people. And I have a passion for seeing them run through life's storms to become who life called them to be. For now, I had nothing left to give for the day. All I wanted to do was indulge in self care, write, pray, and sleep.

That evening, I received a message from my supervisor.

"I'm so proud of how you handled today," she texted. "Before you interviewed with our office, the staff questioned if you were a good fit for the position," I told her that didn't surprise me.

They didn't know, but I felt the same way when I interviewed.

My supervisor said she spoke up for me without knowing me because she knew that what I'd gone through qualified me to speak with people who had no more fight within.

"Remember, don't stress without a place to release it," she texted again. "You are too strong to quit." She also reminded me to never leave God out of where He sent me because I'd need Him when I got there.

"Thank you," I texted back, and then I laid down and stared at the ceiling.

Those words from her will always stick close to me, because as we said our good-nights, at ten o'clock, my phone rang and everything about that day shattered my fragile heart.

HUPOMONE

"Amber, where are you?" Eloise asked me, her voice trembling on the phone.

"I'm in my room," I said. "Is everything okay? I can't handle anything else today."

"It's Sayge. She tried to kill herself today," she said.

With my heart racing, I threw my body out of bed, grabbed my keys, and went home to Birmingham. I wept that entire drive back home because that morning, the feeling I got was for *this* moment.

Around lunch that day, I texted Sayge for the first time in months, and I got no response. I didn't even know why I was texting her.

Sayge and I grew up in the same city. We had similar backgrounds that made us relatable, and we were just two people trying to understand life and be something in life.

At the time, our friendship went back eight years, and we knew everything about each other. But somewhere in that time frame, distance grew between us, and we stopped talking. In part because I couldn't grasp some hard truths about myself. Not being able to accept myself put a wedge in our friendship, and as a result, I ran.

I figured Sayge was busy when I texted her, and considering it'd been months since we spoke, she probably wasn't concerned with texting me back.

It was near midnight when I approached those brown double doors in the hospital. Families had made a home out of the waiting room. Not knowing who they were waiting for or why, I remembered my family and friends once sat like that, waiting for me.

Before approaching the buzzer to enter the intensive care unit, I leaned my head against a glass window and cried because I felt the emotions others felt all over again.

I rang the buzzer, and the nurse told me that visitors weren't allowed after nine o'clock. I understood the hospital had rules, but I needed to go back there. I wanted to give a rebuttal. I wanted to ring the buzzer again. I wanted to be *that* person, but I didn't want to be *that* person. I told the nurse I understood, and I walked away.

Getting to the end of the hallway, the nurse approached the door again and yelled for me to come back.

"Excuse me, ma'am, I don't know you, but something is telling me to let you back here," she said. So she did. That was nobody but God.

I entered Sayge's room with hurt for her resting on my shoulders. As I looked at her, I had no words, and neither did she, so we sat in silence for a few minutes.

Five minutes passed when Sayge looked at me and started crying.

"Amber, I'm tired," she said as the tears fell from her eyes.

I didn't say a word. Even though I didn't know why she was tired, a part of me understood her tiredness because I was once tired.

"Who told you what happened to me, and how did you get back here?" she asked, eyes red and heavy.

"Why didn't you respond to my message earlier today?" I responded, hoping she'd give me an answer.

"I saw your text message, but I couldn't respond because the moment you texted me, I was writing my goodbye letter. I knew you would've tried to make me change my mind if I responded to you," she said, clearly knowing me.

I couldn't say anything else.

I sat back there with Sayge for about thirty more minutes, hoping she'd understand she wasn't -- and never would -- be alone.

I entered my dorm room early that morning and fell to the floor. I lay on the carpet in a puddle of tears.

In twenty-four hours, I'd been in the hospital encouraging a student and in another hospital praying that my friend would make it out on the other side. Something about these hospital events, reminding me of me, had turned the mirror on me from when I was at the lowest point in my life. I learned that what I'd gone through, and will continue to go through, was to encourage someone else.

As an intern, it was clear that I needed to go back even further to where all my hurt started. And that was the death of my best friend and the day we celebrated her life.

So mentally, I went back.

When I parked on the curb across the street from Porcia's house the day we celebrated her life, I cried and screamed, begging God to help me make sense of this loss. I was hurting in a way that I'd never hurt before.

After an hour of hyperventilating in my car, I asked God one last time to help me understand why she left so soon.

Although I didn't know what I was waiting for, I waited. I didn't want to miss whatever *this* was.

After wiping the tears from my eyes, God told me to look at her SUV one more time. I turned my head and noticed a word on her back car tag I'd never seen before.

HUPOMON
(hoop-om-on-ay)

"Now, Porcia, what is this unusual-looking word you've got on the back of your tag?" I wondered, asking Porcia and laughing at the same time.

I sat in my car, red-faced and puzzled because I'd never heard this word before. I was looking up the meaning of a word I couldn't even pronounce.

Hupomone is a Greek word that means to be steadfast, to persevere, and to endure. It's the willingness to go under trial and stay there because you know that God is with you and He'll carry you through. There is no understanding of why things are happening the way they are, but you know that if you endure, it'll build you, and you'll learn what you need for where you are going. It is seeing the storm and choosing to run straight through it, no matter how bad it gets, because you know there is purpose on the other side.

I sat there in silence.

I stared at my phone and then Porcia's car.

This revelation hit me like a ton of bricks.

As I went back mentally, it all started making sense.

I allowed the storms of my life - hurt and pain - to stand in the way of my purpose in life. I tasted pain, shame, and regret to the point where I was unknowingly dependent on it. Those things allowed me to hide behind what I'd done and what happened to me and stopped me from experiencing the fullness of life.

I was ready to own my story and embrace my purpose.

I prepared to be the woman I already was deep down inside, and "to be" meant I had to accept every beautiful and ugly part of me. There'd be a cost, and although I didn't know how much I'd have to pay, I'd been enduring through life since I came out of Momma's womb. Enduring, persevering, and remaining steadfast is all I know.

Porcia was gone, and it all began to make sense, six years later.

I was Hupomone. That was the collateral beauty.

ON A CHILLY NIGHT IN DECEMBER 2016, I deleted my first-ever blog, *essaysforhisglory.com*, a blog I created because people didn't enjoy my more extended essays on social media. I hadn't entirely severed the tie between people-bondage and myself, so I started something that held me back.

After deleting it, I created *thehupomone.com*, the start of stepping into *my* purpose. It was humbling, mind-blowing, and unreal. It felt good and it was right.

The following day, I made one of the last cups of coffee I'd ever make on that campus. I sat on my bedroom floor, drinking my coffee, and reflecting on my time at UA in my blush pink journal.

Afterward, I whipped up some cheesy eggs, fried some crispy bacon, and finished with some buttery toast.

I walked to the community room and sat in that same brown chair where I sat with Saire. I ate my breakfast in silence and took everything from my time at UA in.

HUPOMONE

I got up and looked out the window, and the tears rolled down my face. As I caught them, I remembered that I was human, and even when I was weak, because of God, I was strong. He had carried me through those five and a half years.

After I ate my breakfast, I got my makeup done.

I stepped into my soft-toned, lavender, baby blue, and cream-colored dress that hugged the figure I once found my identity. I slid my feet into my nude six-inch heels and put on the cap and gown I never thought I'd wear. I strutted across that campus one last time, smiling big like my Daddy.

I sat in the Coleman Coliseum in awe of how I got there and was really there. I couldn't do anything but thank God because I wouldn't have made it without Him.

Standing at the bottom of the stairs connected to the stage, I glanced at the crowd.

I walked up the stairs and handed the man the white card with my name. As he said my name and signaled for me to walk across the stage, tears rolled down my eyes.

I saw my granddaddy, Daddy's Dad, sitting next to Daddy, who whistled loudly. As my whole family smiled and waved, my granddaddy's smile took me back to the words he said when he walked me down the field for Homecoming Court – *don't let go of God's unchanging hands.*

I held on to God's unchanging hands and stepped back into Amber Nicole Underwood.

While I accomplished much on paper for those five and a half years, the work done within me made this journey worth it all.

I learned what it meant to fight through life as I healed, and though I sometimes failed, I found the courage to get up and try again.

I learned how to laugh and smile again and began to love who God created me to be. I led several women in small groups, failing at that tremendously too. But I learned to lead and love well, first taking care of myself.

I gained friends who instilled in me the importance of acknowledgment, attention, communication, and enduring.

Everything I became resulted from allowing myself to go through my process with God, even when I didn't understand it.

Five and a half years of surrendering and learning that I hadn't yet arrived. Five and a half years of learning to understand that my degree was less about how much money I'd make and more about who I'd become.

Two days later, I said goodbye to the seventh floor of Presidential Village, and I left a piece of my heart at the University of Alabama, *"where legends are made."*

In Loving Memory of:
Grandaddy John Henry Cohill, July 10, 1947 – January 20, 2016
Bradley Morris, June 22, 1993 - February 1, 2016
FabryeAnne Robinson, July 1, 1990 – May 8, 2016

9

Unknown

I GRADUATED FROM COLLEGE and thought I'd go back to school to get my master of business administration degree, get established in my career, get married, and have tons of kids. But in my last semester of college, I traded my plans for God's plans, and His plans led me to a place called the unknown – the Dominican Republic.

I knew I was going to the Dominican Republic, and I'd be there for six months, but some of me didn't know what I was thinking. I don't know how I said yes, because the unknown is where not many choose to go.

Sure, I'd been to the Dominican Republic twice but this time my going there was different.

I don't know how I went from being a type-A planner who needed all the details to becoming a risk-taker who didn't care what I left behind. But there I was. It was just me, God, and His directions.

One month after graduation, I let go of the life I once wanted and traded six months of my life for foreign soil.

Two weeks before I left for the Dominican Republic, my reality started to set in. I'd always been bold in where God told me to go, but I started feeling everything on the other side of the world before I got there.

My car gave out again, and people's fears about my decision started scaring me. For a moment, I took my eyes off what God told me to do and became concerned with the opinions of others.

Was it unwise to dismiss "corporate America" and serve in a country with no pay?

Was the little Spanish I knew enough to help me communicate there?

Was I going to get sick and develop a life-threatening illness?

Would the water give me parasites?

Would the color of my skin cause individuals to treat me differently?

Would my things get stolen?

Would I lose my friends because of my absence?

These questions plagued me, and the truth was, all those things could happen to me right there in Alabama.

I couldn't answer the questions because I didn't know what was next. I was ashamed to say that what God called me to do didn't even make sense to me. It all came down to one question: *would I do what God told me to do, even if no one supported me?*

I had to shut down the opinions of others and realize I owed no one an explanation. I wanted to walk by Faith. I got tired of searching for God when my plans failed, so I searched for Him before creating them.

Everyone around me told me to stay home, but everything inside me said go.

This trip wasn't a checkbox to check off on a bucket list. I was doing something bigger than myself, not to yield a badge of honor, but to obey what God said to do. I knew I had free will, but I wanted the freedom that led me to His will for my life. So I sold all the heels where I found my internal worth, secured my monthly financial donors, and said my goodbyes.

Three suitcases and two carry-ons later, I went *back* to the Dominican Republic for the third time in less than two years. Coming from where I'm from, that was unheard of.

———

AROUND TWO O'CLOCK ON A Tuesday in January 2017, I landed in the Dominican Republic. I picked up my phone and sent a mass text to my family and friends, telling them I'd made it safely. I filled out the blue customs form with my favorite black pen and handed it back to the flight attendant. I got off the plane and texted my uncle, then my phone died.

The night before I left, Caitlin asked for my prayer requests. I must've been high off anticipation because I didn't understand the weight of the prayer request I gave her: *"Please pray that I'd be open to anything that would stretch me the minute I get off the plane."*

When my phone died, my thoughts raced.

What was I thinking?
What did I say yes to?
Why did I agree to this?

The truth was that growing and being stretched was a byproduct of me saying yes. I wasn't exempt from being tested because I said yes to God. In fact, I like to think that because I said yes, I signed myself up to go through more. You bet over the next six months, growth was waiting for me.

I wasn't coming to serve; I was coming to *be served*.

"Welcome home, Amber," my boss said, who was the director of the school I'd serve. He and his wife were smiling so big, and I was irritated. I slapped a fake smile on my face because, while I was excited to be back in the Dominican Republic, all I could think about was what Momma was thinking. My phone was dead, and I knew she was losing it on the other side of the world.

"Hola," I replied, with my emotions all over the place.

"You're finally back," he replied, putting all my bags into his truck. I looked up at the clear skies, trying to put my irritation to the side, and took in the moment.

My boss and his wife spoke into my life on my second mission trip to the Dominican Republic in 2015. They saw

UNKNOWN

me working with a group of young girls there for a season. My return was ordained. And regardless of what was happening upon my arrival, I was back and had to be *there*.

As we pulled out of the airport and onto the road leading me to where I'd be staying for the next six months, I noticed not much had changed.

Potholes still riddled the roads, and my head still hit the window a few times. The villages were just as rural as when I first came, and the air was still thick and unpleasant. The fields were still open and expansive, the palm trees were still beautiful, and the women walked down the streets holding baskets on their heads. While not much had changed, nothing felt the same.

Ten minutes had gone by, and we pulled up to a two-story white building that housed four apartments.

As we turned on the street Tierra Dominicana to my apartment, I remembered I'd been on that street before.

When I came to the Dominican Republic two years prior, I watched a group of men work on my apartment complex. If you had told me I'd live in one of those apartments, I would've laughed. Because the idea of living in another country, let alone my own place, was impossible to *me*.

My apartment was on the second floor, shut in by a set of black jail bars. I was the new kid on the block, and everyone stood in the streets watching me. I didn't know if this was a good thing or a bad thing, but before my thoughts could get the best of me, these little perky voices, screaming my name, grabbed my attention.

"Amber, tu regresaste y no mentiste," screamed Rose and Brandy, wearing their school uniforms and the cutest smiles I hadn't seen in a long time.

According to them, I was back, and I didn't lie.

I met the girls a year before in my second time in the Dominican Republic. So much happened in my time away from the Dominican Republic that I don't even recall telling them I was coming back. But I was back.

"Si, mi ninas," I replied, telling them yes and giving them hugs as tears fell from all of our eyes.

I told them I had a lot to do, but we had nothing but time to spend together in the coming days.

Later that day, my boss, his wife, and I returned to my new home after purchasing what I needed to start in my first apartment.

My apartment was white on the outside with a big brown door. It had two bedrooms, one bathroom, a walk-in closet, a living room, a kitchen, and a dining area that led to a balcony. It was a small apartment, and I made it into everything I ever wanted in my own home.

I took a moment, lying on my living room floor and cried. I had the keys to my first apartment, and it was in another country. Those years of sharing a room with my sister and roommates humbled me, and I wanted nothing more than to open up my home to others.

I must've been on that floor for an hour or two because when I got up, I walked out on my balcony and noticed the sun was going down. I walked to the light switch to turn the lights on, but when I flicked the lights, the lights didn't come on. I knew I didn't have power at certain times throughout the day, but I didn't expect it to be this day, on my first day there.

I walked to my landlord's home next door to get assistance and clarity on what I needed to do. After an hour of fiddling around with the lights, my landlord's son restored the power.

My cell phone had been dead for about eight hours, so I plugged it in the outlet and finished making my new apartment home. After two hours of unpacking and cleaning, I turned my phone on to call Momma, who I knew was ready to make me come back home. When I got to my phone, I noticed the white apple was just staring back at me.

I'd plugged in my phone for at least two hours; it should've worked. I tried everything I knew to make it come on, including putting it in rice, but nothing worked. My brand new iPhone 6 crashed on my first day in another country, which shouldn't have been a problem because I was a pro at cutting my phone off with purpose, but it was.

I laid down that night, frightened and upset. As I lay there, I talked with God, looking up at my ceiling, and it went something like this...

"God, I know I said yes," I told Him. *"But is this what this journey will be like because I want to go home if it is. I'm in another country, and I need to know if you're with me because if you're not, I want to leave."*

At that moment, I remembered that some of the most committed people live their lives in unforeseen circumstances. I said I am sold-out for the will of God for my life, but I couldn't help but wonder if I was more committed to God or the comfort of my phone.

I had a choice. I didn't have to be there, but I stayed because God had always put me in places that would make me better. I forced myself to find rest in the midst of it all.

Those days without my cell phone brought an uncomfortable truth – *I didn't know where I placed my security until it was no longer accessible to me.*

My boss took me to a local phone repair shop a few days later, where I got my phone fixed for twenty dollars. After turning it on, calling Momma, and checking over one hundred messages, I couldn't wait to tell the people following my journey about my apartment and that my heart couldn't contain the gratitude I had for it. So I posed in front of my building and posted the picture on social media.

A few hours after posting my photo, I received a message on Instagram from a woman named April. She told me she served in the same city and thought we should meet up. I didn't know if she was real or if this was a scam, but that evening I took a motoconcho to her side of town and learned that April was real.

April was a black woman in her early thirties who left her high-paying job to serve in the Dominican Republic. She invited me into her home, and we got to know each other over coffee and cookies. Her home was inviting, and the aesthetics made me want to go to Ikea. I was in a safe place.

"So tell me what brought you here?" she asked me.

"Different things that happened in my life brought me here," I said. "But most importantly, I'm being obedient to God." After telling each other about who we were, she invited me to do life with her while I was there.

When I took her up on that offer, I had no idea that I was walking into another level of seeing myself. We were both forced to face the cultural discomforts that being in the Dominican Republic brought.

My first week in the Dominican Republic brought unexpected experiences. I was able to sit in my living room on the floor and eat grilled cheese sandwiches with six little girls. I began teaching a young lady English, and in return, she taught me more Spanish. I shared a conversation with someone of a different religion in a local coffee shop. The discussion was meaningful because it taught me the importance of sitting with people who don't live or look like you, and have different belief systems; everyone has a story and we are all humans.

Although I wanted to give up because of my lack of communication with my family and friends back home, and lack of power, it wasn't my nature to walk away. I was in the Dominican Republic for a reason. It'd get more challenging, but God's grace covered me.

———

It was a hot, muggy Sunday morning when the roosters outside my bedroom window woke me up.

I got up and brewed a cup of black Dominican coffee. If I was excited about any aspect of returning to the Dominican Republic, it was to drink their rich, smooth, and tasty coffee. I was already a coffee addict, and their coffee didn't make it better. You know it's good when you don't need any cream or sugar.

As I slurped the coffee around in my mouth, I pondered what to eat for breakfast. All I wanted was an avocado to pair with my cheesy eggs. I hadn't yet familiarized myself with the city so I had no idea where to get an avocado. I stood on my balcony and analyzed the streets to see who could help me find one.

My landlord came out of her house and took a seat on her front porch. I took this as an invitation to spark a conversation.

"Buenos dias," I greeted her, nervous about my Spanish not being correct or good enough. She smiled at me and told me good morning back.

"Tú sabes dónde puedo comprar un abogado?" I asked, hoping she could understand what I was asking and tell me where to buy an avocado.

Immediately, her eyes grew to be the size of jawbreakers. She was already shorter than me, with a petite build, so I got worried when her eyes got big.

"Yo dije algo malo?" I asked her, trying to see if I said something wrong.

"No," she said, waving her hands for one of the neighbors to come over.

The man from across the street stood there with us, trying to understand what I wanted. At this point, everyone on my street stood outside their homes, staring in my direction.

UNKNOWN

"Amber, no entendemos porqué necesitas un abogado," he said, trying to understand why I needed an avocado.

Something wasn't adding up.

"Yo quiero una abogado por mi desayuno," I replied, frustrated because all I told them was that I wanted to buy an avocado to go with my breakfast.

The man told me I wouldn't find an "abogado" in my town, and the ones for sale were expensive. None of this made sense because I knew that if there were any avocados here, they had to be in my town.

"Yo no entiendo," I said to him. I didn't understand. Not only had I drawn attention to myself, but it turns out that I didn't know what I was asking for.

"Tu quieres un abogado o un aguacate?" he said, trying to gain clarity on what I wanted again.

I was under the impression that I asked for an avocado, but I actually asked for a lawyer. It turned out I had my words mixed up, big time.

My jaws grew tight, and my back tensed up. I was embarrassed.

"Ahhh. Yo quiero un aguacate. Gracias por tu ayuda," I said, telling them thank you.

I walked back up the stairs to my apartment. I plopped down on my floor, and for a split second, I was frustrated. But instead, I laughed. I didn't have the time to wallow in self-pity when I had months to get better in my Spanish. So I cooked my eggs, and instead of an avocado, I had a handful of strawberries and almonds.

I made my to-do list for the week and immersed myself in the Dominican culture.

My first stop was back to my landlords to discuss my bills. I didn't have an accurate concept of money, and this was my first time paying my bills, so I wanted to make sure that I began the right way. My rent, including water, was two hundred dollars. My power and gas bill averaged about fifteen to twenty dollars a month based on what I used for the month. I also had to factor in my grocery and transportation bill.

Afterward, I walked the community's streets to familiarize myself with the local grocery store and the supermarket. It turned out that I didn't need to walk far to either one because anything I needed was sold next door or across the street in someone's home.

I noticed the women took care of their homes and worked in the family store. It was like clockwork. By five o'clock in the morning their husbands were gone, and an hour later, the store opened. Some nights, I wondered if they slept because they stayed open late.

I didn't see many fast-food restaurants, and almost everything was grown locally. I became a student of learning how to cook Dominican dishes, and Pinterest became my best friend.

After walking the streets for a few weeks, I saw pigs get slaughtered, hung from hooks, and sold. As the chickens were caught in bags and sold, their crying haunted me at night and woke me in the mornings. So I attempted to go vegan because of what I saw in the streets. While that decision was short-lived and brought me great health benefits, I had to understand my body, and it wanted chicken.

As I made my way to one of the many padadas, something like bus stops, I saw a gym. Buying a gym membership for one month was only seven dollars. The endless amounts of rice and beans I ate caused me to gain that freshman fifteen weight again, so I made sure to get a membership to at least stay toned up.

As I waited for my guagua to arrive, I noticed there were three forms of transportation: guaguas, motoconchos, and carritos. The guaguas were vans and the cheapest but slowest form of transportation. The conductor stands at the door to let passengers on and off the van. They collect the money and tell the driver where the passengers need to go. The vans make stops until filled.

The motoconchos, motorcycles were common transportation and the most dangerous. The drivers drove fast and often without helmets. Most people in the city made money driving a motoconcho.

The carritos, taxis carried fewer people. Depending on the driver and his carrito, two people rode in the passenger seat, and five people sat in the backseat. Carritos provided ease that guaguas didn't.

I took my first guagua into the city, a carrito back into town, and I rode a motoconcho from the bus stop, home. Taking a ride in all three came with one valuable lesson: *I shouldn't pass judgment on a culture I'd never experienced before.*

I came home to a knock at my door from a woman I met when I first went to the Dominican Republic in 2015. Word must've gotten around fast that I was back because I didn't tell her I was back. She was our cook on my previous trips, and when I tell you she can cook, she can cook. I'm talking about good cooking, like my grandma.

I opened the door to her, still wearing her long skirts, hair pulled back in a low bun, and her chocolate brown skin glowing as it always did. She reminded me of Momma, somehow knowing my every move. Not to mention she lived a block away from me.

"Amber, tu eres aqui mi niña," she said, stretching her arms to hug me and showing all her teeth because she was happy I was there.

"Siiiiiiiii mama," I replied, hugging her like a kid hugging their grandma.

"Amber, vengo a enseñarte cómo hacer La Bandera," she insisted that I get in the kitchen and learn how to make the traditional Dominican dish (rice, beans, and fried plantains, with an avocado).

"Yo estoy lista," I replied, telling her I was ready to learn.

That night, I sat on my living room floor eating this dish with Rose, Dory, Dani, Brandy, Lisa, and Ada, six little girls I claimed as my little sisters.

My stomach and heart were full, and I was content. I belonged there.

A few weeks went by when I turned on the water to take a shower and nothing came out of the faucet. I went

UNKNOWN

next door to my landlord to ask her what I needed to do, and she told me I didn't have the traditional water system.

Every week, two men added water to the tinaco tank that sat on my roof, a tank that served as the water source to my apartment. After learning that I could run out of water, I bought several five-gallon water jugs to keep nearby.

My laundry days consisted of an oversized purple bowl to hand wash all my clothes. After washing them, I walked to my roof and pinned them to the line to dry.

The little girls I fellowshipped with taught me that I knew very little about serving. Watching them wash my dishes and showing me how to double bag old food before throwing it away so it wouldn't smell as bad -- both without being asked -- showed me I could use more lessons on serving.

My idea of being on time was wrecked when I learned that the concept of time there was different from mine. And no matter how strategically I organized my days, they often didn't go as planned. This organizing took some time to get used to because the type A in me wasn't happy.

Every day at lunch, the people who had businesses inside their homes shut their doors for a few hours to enjoy lunch with their families. Lunch was considered the biggest and most important meal of the day. Lunch was my favorite meal because it was a meal that often put me to sleep, and I love to sleep.

I understood that poverty wasn't a way of life but rather a passed down or learned mindset.

While these families didn't have much to others, they had the same amount of time in the day as me, and they made the most of their days: they woke up early and worked until finished for that day.

My appearance was meaningful to people there, and if I ever looked unkept, someone made sure to tell me how I looked. Every day I learned something new about myself.

On the days I struggled to make my apartment feel like a home - when the temperature was fiery inside, there was no water, and my food was spoiled because of power outages - I gazed at the name of my street, Tierra Dominicana. April told me that it meant I was figuratively and literally on Dominican soil. Knowing that, I consciously chose to connect with where I was by allowing myself to feel my emotions as I weaved my way through being there.

Monday through Friday, I served as an administrative assistant to my boss, and on Saturdays, I worked alongside teachers in their classrooms. I was a kid magnet, and the kids reminded me to keep the main thing the main thing - wonder.

The mission of Metro West Caribbean Mission was to develop a community where people were fed, educated, and equipped with the skills needed to go further in life. I assisted my boss and the teachers I worked alongside to ensure we did precisely that.

We created a holistic curriculum for teachers. I walked through the community to better understand its working and surveyed its condition. Walking in the community allowed me to build relationships with people, like the men of the fire department, who looked after me daily. They asked me if I needed anything and wanted me to tell them if anyone bothered me or made me feel uncomfortable.

At the time, the organization was going through a transition, which was a challenge, but I did what I could with what I had.

One week, I spent two days researching how to create the best inventory sheet for the school. Between the research I did and my creativity, I thought the one I made was stellar. I printed the sheets with confidence and gave them to my boss. What I wasn't ready for was his response.

"These are great, but there is more in you. These sheets can be better," my boss said, giving them back to me.

I just looked at him. Offended deep down inside, I realized I'd absolutely been corrected professionally, in a manner that my superiors hadn't in a while.

I thought what I created was excellent, but he saw a need for it to be better, and he made me go back to fix it. He saw something in me much more significant than what I was producing for the school, and he did everything he could to nurture that.

I was on training ground and I had to suit up because this journey continued to show me that I hadn't arrived.

Nevertheless, I was ready to get off work and go home that day.

That evening, I laid on my couch and processed that day and the days prior. One lesson rang true - I was being emptied of myself professionally, culturally, relationally, and financially.

I was going back to face the honest Amber, the Amber that grew up in the trailer.

10

Emptied

It was warm and sunny outside when I took a seat on my balcony. My glass door was wide open, and my gray curtains flowed out the balcony window. The smell of garbage, mixed with flowers and rain, filled my apartment. My computer was on my lap, a book sat on the side of my white plastic chair, and I held a fresh cup of black coffee in my right hand.

The roosters crowed loudly as they always did, and two dogs barked with fury as the motoconcho made its way down the street.

Dory hung on the rails of my balcony as if she was on the edge of the ship *Titanic*. Rose sat next to me on the floor, writing in a journal because she wanted to write like me.

As I looked behind me into my home, I noticed the little feet imprinted on my white tile kitchen floor, marking the place where the little girls found joy in my apartment. Brandy and Ada pieced together a Barbie puzzle on the kitchen floor, laughing and having the time of their lives.

After Rose finished writing in her journal, she ran back inside my apartment. She insisted I stay in my seat because she had a surprise for me.

I stayed there.

Rose yelled for me to close my eyes, and as I closed my eyes, the sound of heels came clacking across my floor closer to me.

Rose told me to open my eyes, and when I did, she had on my black, six-inch heels, the one pair of heels I owned there.

She took a curtsy in my heels and fell.

After I helped her up and made sure she was okay, I went back to my balcony and stood there. Looking down the street, that moment brought back an old memory.

Rose was me when I was a little girl in the trailer.

Seeing myself in Rose in those heels did something to me, so I sent the girls home, and I went to a juice spot in a neighboring town for some alone time.

After I placed my order for a green smoothie, I got sick. I'd just eaten, so if I was ill, the only thing I could think of was the food not settling well in my stomach.

Physically, my body rejected what I ate. After letting go of it all, I returned to my apartment.

The beaming rays from the sun heated the water tank on my roof. Hot water wasn't something I controlled with

EMPTIED

a knob-like I was used to, so I was thankful for a hot shower, a small luxury I had there.

As I stood under the shower, I noticed my menstrual cycle had started. The water faded out and then stopped, leaving me covered in soap. I stood under the showerhead screaming because my water went in and out for two consecutive days, and of *all* days, my water ran out. I was emotional.

I dried my tears and stepped out of the shower to fill my pots with water. The water I had was my drinking water. I poured it into the pots and boiled it on the stove.

I had no tub, so I dipped my rag in the pots and bathed myself. All I could think about was being a little girl in the trailer again, boiling water for my bath in the winter. Even though none of this was foreign to me, I couldn't help but wonder why I was back *here* again.

My open balcony door reminded me of the screen door at the trailer in the summer. My apartment was made of concrete and had no solid infrastructure, which reminded me of the hot days in the trailer. I remained cool by getting low and lying on my apartment floor, as I didnt have an air conditioning unit. Getting down and lying there reminded me of how quickly God can humble me.

I went to sleep sweating and woke up sweating.

After a while, all I wanted was cold showers.

After two days of boiling water and bathing out of cooking pots, I woke up to the sound of my water running in the bathroom.

I was thankful to have running water again.

HUPOMONE

The following Saturday morning, I brewed a hot cup of cinnamon and nutmeg coffee and ate my breakfast. The sun shined through my balcony window in a way I hadn't seen since I first arrived. It was glistening yellow, and I could feel the heat sweep over my body.

I plopped down in my chair at the bar and checked my emails before going to work. As I scrolled through my inbox, I noticed an email with the subject line, "Invoice from Event."

"Hi, I just want to remind you that you have an outstanding balance with us," the email said.

Why did I have an invoice from a paid event? I wondered.

I stared at the screen, shaking, because not only was the venue paid for, but the company also asked for over seven hundred dollars, the money I didn't have to give them.

I felt like I was drowning in worry and defeat, all while saying yes to God in coming there. I didn't have the mental and emotional energy to overcome one more obstacle by myself. So I took my worry to God in prayer and asked Him what to do.

Before coming to the Dominican Republic, my pastor told me that "faith would always be my currency." So when God told me to pay the money and trust Him with the rest, I did it scared.

Growing up, Momma didn't talk to us about money. She did her best with what she had, and her main concern was making sure we had clothes on our backs and food to

EMPTIED

eat. Daddy didn't teach us about money either, but his work ethic and entrepreneurial mindset were unmatched. They modeled how to show up for work and be resilient in failure. Through the financial crisis I was in, I took both examples and continued to endure. But I needed help knowing how to handle money.

The money I had was for emergencies until I started receiving money from my donors the next month. My faith wavered when I realized I still had two weeks left in that month. I had a little over two dollars in my bank account; nevertheless, I paid my bills.

I had family and friends I could call on, but every time I called someone, "faith is your currency" rang loud in my ears, and a nudge in my spirit kept stopping me.

I never made the calls.

I stood in my kitchen, looking around to see what I had to eat. I had a can of coffee, a pack of ramen noodles, a can of beans, one banana, and a small carton of chocolate milk. I prayed in the middle of my living room floor, asking God where my next meal would come from after eating my ramen noodles and beans for dinner.

I knew God would provide, but I'd be lying if I said I wasn't sure how He would. Changing lives and saying yes was great in theory, but I had questions when I couldn't figure out how to eat.

The following morning, I had my last banana and chocolate milk for breakfast, and I went to work.

Not knowing where the food would come from, I returned home for lunch a few hours later. My stomach was having a full-blown conversation with me, and I had no explanation for what we'd eat.

HUPOMONE

I sat at my bar, drinking another cup of coffee, and just thanked God for what He'd already done in my life.

As I took a cat nap before going back to work, there was a knock at my door.

"Amber, comida para ti," Rose's mom said, standing in my doorway smiling, telling me she brought me food.

I stood there frozen, tears welling up in my eyes and total disbelief.

Before I could say thank you, the tears just rolled down my face.

"Why'd you bring me food?" I asked her in Spanish.

"Dios sabe," she said, telling me God knew.

She handed me the food and made her way back across the street.

I shut my door and fell to my knees because she was right; God knew.

She loaded that plate with chicken, rice, and beans, and I savored every bite, slow and steady, with a face full of tears.

God really did provide for me.

Two hours later, Caitlin sent me money because she said God put it on her heart to give it to me.

Caitlin always knew when something was happening with me, so I wasn't surprised she reached out. She understood my need to be obedient in leaving all that I knew, and she stood by me when most people didn't.

Her challenge to me was to go on a financial fast. On that fast, I had to sit with myself and what I knew about money, allowing God to uproot any financial hang-ups in my life. She encouraged me to face my debt rather than be

EMPTIED

afraid of it and make a plan to tackle it, even if that meant I lived below my means. So I grabbed my fancy black budgeting envelopes, and I faced every debt with my name.

I witnessed God provide me with food and eight-hundred dollars, more than what the company asked for, in seven days.

While what I experienced was hard, I continued to see how facing myself was good for me.

A few days later, I headed out into the city for my Spanish class. As I passed by a local barbershop, the barber stepped out and called for me to come back.

"Where are you from?" he asked me, speaking English eloquently well. He was confidently stout with a tummy to match. He had a gelled slick back hairstyle and a clean face.

"I am from the United States of America," I replied.

"Ahhhh. Okay,""I knew you weren't from here because your eyebrows are bushy; you need to get them done," he said, speaking an unapologetic truth about my eyebrows.

How dare he talk about me like that? He doesn't know me, I said to myself, giving him an attitude in my head.

I just stood there looking at him.

"It's okay, I take care of your eyebrows for you for free," he said, smiling and serious about me not looking like what I was going through.

During that time, depending on God to provide, He showed me that He still cares about the little things. I was thankful to have food in my stomach and my eyebrows done.

When I arrived back home that evening, I pulled out Dave Ramsey's, *The Total Money Makeover*, the book

HUPOMONE

Leslie gave me from the women's mission trip. That book helped me get to the root of the problem and guided me on how to stop making excuses about what I could change. I worked with what I had, set a budget, and decided to sit monthly with my finances.

It was early February when I saw a Facebook message from Jeremiah.

"Don't I know you?" he began the message.

"I don't think so, but my name is Amber," I replied, interested in the random conversation.

We were both creative writers who had a heart for words. He seemed more mature than I in the field of writing, and honestly, I just wanted to learn from him.

"I'm sending you three of my books. I'd love your feedback," Jeremiah's message continued. I couldn't help but wonder why I got his books for free, but I read them and gave him my feedback.

After doing so, that was the end of that conversation; nothing more and nothing less.

He messaged me again that March; I was interested in knowing what he wanted to talk about this time.

Our conversation began with small talk, but then he asked me a question that changed the dynamic of everything.

"Amber, are you afraid of romance?" his message read. I was startled that he knew something about me that I'd never told him. I was afraid of romance and He shouldn't have known this.

EMPTIED

"Why do you ask?" I responded, considering we'd never talked about love or relationships. After a while, it became clear that Jeremiah was attempting to pursue me.

Initially, it wasn't his looks that attracted me. It was his love for God and his purpose, heart for people, and the gift of writing. Our conversations were deep, and his words intrigued me.

"I know you. You are the woman I wrote about in my books," he said with confidence, which tripped me up and left me with questions.

How was he so sure of this and is this why he sent me his books? I wondered.

We knew each other from a conversation via social media and the telephone, so it threw me off when he stated he *knew* me. After all, he didn't know me.

"How are you so sure of this?" I asked, needing more clarity on what he strongly felt. Again, we'd never met or been close, but he swore he sensed me coming near him before I was close.

He knew it was weird for him to pursue me online the way he did, but he also thought a woman like me might let him in. And for a split second, I did.

Not long after he told me I was his "wife," -- although we were never legally married or knew anything about each other -- he went silent; in one day, he was gone. He blocked me from all his social media sites, and everything he felt I was to him was over. He was gone and gave me no explanation. He ghosted me.

I racked my brain around Jeremiah's pursuit of me. But I couldn't understand how someone could ask questions and throw words around and not show up in action.

He had done this to how many other women? I wondered.

After weeks of silence from the man who said he was my husband, my phone rang. When he called me, I saw right through him because a person sure of what God told them doesn't play games like these, which was on me, because he never said God told him I was his wife.

Jeremiah apologized for lying to me.

Not long after our last conversation, I saw on Facebook that Jeremiah had gotten married, which told me everything I needed to know about him: he was sneaky, unsure of himself, unsure of what he wanted, and good at running games.

I wasn't hurt; I was amused.

It's amusing that this had happened to me. That stuff like this actually happens to people. I should've been more discerning.

But to answer his first question, I *was* afraid of romance because, like others before him, he showed me that love was nothing more than a game.

Was Jeremiah at fault? Of course, he was, but I was too. I didn't seek God and discern what was of Him and what wasn't.

Jeremiah didn't *see* me, and he didn't *know* me. He studied the type of woman I was, the kind of woman he knew he wanted. I wasn't his, and he wasn't mine.

I was tired of letting the words of a man tell me how worthy I was to be loved. I was tired of falling for relationships and situation-ships that weren't supposed to go as far as they did. So I went back to look at myself in love again.

I knew what I wanted in love. I had to be okay with being misunderstood for wanting a different kind of story, being seen patiently, found in the unraveling, and loved unconditionally even on the hard days.

I had to be okay with doing the work and waiting so that I could have love and see love in its most authentic and honest form.

WHEN I CHOSE TO NO LONGER LIVE a traditional life after graduation, I opened myself up to see more of what prevented me from being my most authentic self.

I was a black woman with a strong personality who was learning herself and still learning to love herself before anyone else could. I had to see myself worthy of respect, love, and honor without a partner. My view of self stemmed from what took root in middle school.

When I was in middle school, the hot guys always went after the lighter-skinned girls with straight hair, which was one of the reasons why I wanted my hair straight in middle school. Natural curly hair was not the "thing," and people gossiped behind your back if you had it. After transitioning from permed hair back to my natural hair in college, I felt insecure.

My fear of getting darker while in the Dominican Republic also stopped me from wearing my hair naturally.

I hadn't yet dealt with this hair insecurity, not as I thought. So April partnered with me, and we went on a journey of becoming comfortable in our brown skin and natural hair.

Being in the Dominican Republic as a single woman always brought questions from the locals. Living alone was not the same as me living alone in Alabama in the culture there. Questions like, "do you live with your husband or parents" were never-ending.

When I told someone I lived alone, they asked if I had moved out of my Momma's house to do things I couldn't do in her home. After explaining why I was there and how our cultures are different, it was clear that we were all culture shocked.

I noticed that I wasn't the only one who didn't want to wear my natural hair. It was universal amongst some women of African descent. There was fear in wearing what we were born with because we didn't fit the mold of what "pretty" was. Society deeming my hair ugly for so long caused me to resort to hairstyles that fit its definition of beautiful.

As I wore my natural hair, the remarks - your hair is too big, too short, or not straight enough – hurt. Becoming me with my natural hair required more out of me. But it was necessary for my personal growth because it allowed me to see myself beyond my skin color and hair texture.

The questions didn't cease, and the remarks intensified as people tried to understand why I was becoming comfortable in my natural self. I went from becoming confident in my roots to having to defend my roots, literally and figuratively. It was exhausting.

EMPTIED

April reminded me of a fundamental truth on the days I wanted to take it personally.

"Amber, remember their comments aren't personal," she said. "It's all cultural, and no matter what, you have to celebrate yourself on the good hair days and the bad hair days, regardless of what anyone thinks."

In the wake of accepting my hair, April, a local Dominican friend, and I took a trip to Santo Domingo to get our hair done.

This hair salon was one of *the* dopest hair salons I'd ever seen. It smelled like Eloise's salon, laced with scents and views of the Dominican Republic.

Music blared from the corners of each wall, and salon operators laid out books on the tables. Behind the receptionist's desk were hair products that I thought you could only find in the United States, and considering I ran out of mine, I made a few purchases.

They had a coffee bar where you could purchase anything from coffee to salads to smoothies. It wasn't your average hair salon. I was getting my hair done at Miss Rizo's! The salon was everything I was looking for and everything my hair needed.

At the time, I'd been natural for three years. Instead of chopping my hair off, I transitioned, allowing the chemicals to grow out of my hair. I trimmed it myself if I ever needed a trim because I was afraid it wouldn't grow back. That's why I shouldn't have been surprised when the stylist stared at my blow-dried-out hair the way she did.

She asked me why one side of my hair was longer than the other. I sat in her chair in tears because I knew I was

HUPOMONE

about to have to get my hair cut. I was starting to accept my hair, only to realize it wasn't healthy.

I held back my tears as I heard the scissors chopping off pieces of my identity. I watched my dead ends drift to the floor, and all I wanted was to cry. The extensions I wore shielded and protected me for so long. Now my hair was falling to the floor, leaving me exposed.

I didn't want to get my hair cut. But for my roots to grow, I knew that my dead ends needed a trim. The longer I held on to what was already dead, the longer I held myself back from growing. So I stopped my pity party and allowed more growth.

I left Miss Rizo's with healthier hair and emptied out even more.

For as long as I can remember, slavery and the treatment of African Americans led me to believe that being an African American in America was a disgrace. Between those white boys calling me a nigger and the reality of what happened to my ancestors, my skin color showed me the majority sees me as "less than." Grade-school textbooks showed me pictures of my roots. However, they failed to teach me about the physical and mental enslavement my ancestors experienced and how people today still experience it. I could no longer use where I wasn't enlightened as an excuse not to learn what was available.

As I opened myself up to those hard conversations with people in the Dominican Republic, discussions began teaching me the importance of listening before I reply. I began seeking to understand people's backgrounds because where you come from and what you experience shapes who

EMPTIED

you become. My behavior change made it easier to accept someone as he or she was, even if I didn't understand.

On a hot, sweaty Wednesday in March, my boss, his wife, the maintenance guy, and I pulled up to the mission house. We all had different tasks for the day. I had the pleasure of getting my hands dirty by replacing the battery in the truck. I checked the oil and coolant, and I used a scanner to inspect the vehicle for any issues. In the house, I changed the breakers, rewired systems in the walls, and painted bedroom walls. After I finished my work, I went outside to rake leaves.

As I put the dead leaves into the trash can, I noticed three small plants trying to come from under the other leaves surrounding them. I threw the bag of leaves over my shoulder and went up the hill in the backyard to start raking another section. Inclined to look back, I noticed that the once-limp plants had begun to rise. Immediately, God began to speak to me.

He told me that these rising plants were a representation of my life. I had everything I needed to accomplish my purpose, but I remained limp and stuck because I wouldn't remove the things around me that no longer served me. I needed to be intentional about how I lived while I was in the Dominican Republic because once that season was up, there'd be no time to look back.

At this point, I was exhausted from all the internal work taking place. I thought I'd addressed the professional, financial, relational, and cultural sides of myself, so I couldn't understand what more I needed to work on; silly me. But I, too, knew that if I returned to Alabama the same, all my insecurities, doubts, and unbelief would go with me.

My limited access to friends and family forced me to be with God in the secret place, the place where He knew me.

I'd been living out a commercialized gospel. Sugar-coated conversations often filled well-intentioned coffee dates. Snapping a picture of my coffee and journal at the local coffee shop sealed the deal that I'd done my good deed for the day. Being known by people took the place of being known by God. Sunday fashion masked the pain, worries, and insecurities under my clothes. And knowledge of God's Word did me no good if I used His Word to hurt those He called me to love.

My prayers and fasting were so routine that it felt forced and rehearsed when I sat down to talk to God. But what seemed forced and rehearsed was right because I finally became my true self with God.

I abandoned religion because rules led me to believe that legalism was the only way to God. Now, I was in a relationship with Him. Even though I couldn't see Him, I knew He was there, as He'd been all along.

Realizing I didn't have control, I destroyed every thought and idea I had about how those six months in the Dominican Republic would look. However, it wasn't until I left the Dominican Republic - where I did the internal work - and went back to Alabama - where I was to apply the work - that God revealed He'd always have something to teach me.

11

Conscious

I woke up to my six little sisters screaming, "Feliz Cumpleanos Amber," on my twenty-fourth birthday in March. They were outside my balcony, jumping up and down, more excited for my birthday than I was.

I walked into my living room and opened the large cardboard box I'd received from a dear friend back home. When I opened it, I found my favorite things: cookware, gourmet food, chocolate, and a bathrobe with slippers. He really did it up for me with that gift. And then I opened the most unexpected gift - a gift card for time away in Dubai from another friend. After looking through the package and finishing my morning routine, April picked me up for a day at the spa.

HUPOMONE

I got a deep-tissue massage and a much-needed manicure and pedicure. We sat under the pavilion on the beach, staring at the white waves crashing to the shore. I was relaxed and gulped down my virgin Pina colada and guacamole and chips.

I journaled about the previous month and wrote out goals for the next month. After stuffing my face with more food from the spa and watching the sunset, April and I wrapped things up and made our way back to my apartment.

As we turned onto my street, I noticed my six little sisters running toward April's car, dressed in white t-shirts and blue jeans. I don't know if they had a tracker on me or if they had camped out in the neighbor's yard all day, but they rushed April's car like they knew I was coming. I got out of the vehicle with never-ending kisses and hugs.

"Amber, tus ojos," they screamed, which meant they wanted me to close my eyes.

"Que pasa mi niñas," I replied, insisting they tell me what was happening before I covered my eyes.

"No, no, no," they all kept yelling.

I closed my eyes. I wasn't going to open them, but I hoped I didn't trip up the stairs.

"Aqui," they yelled, telling me to stand where they put me in my living room, demanding I don't remove the blindfold from my eyes. I stood there in my long yellow and green floral sundress, waiting for whatever was about to happen.

After seemingly fifteen minutes, they took my blindfold off and immediately started singing so loud.

"Feliz Cumpleanos! Feliz Cumpleanos!" they screamed, singing happy birthday. I cried because these little girls planned a birthday surprise for me.

A rectangular pineapple cake sat gracefully on my bar, and a firecracker-like candle sent out flames from the center of the cake. They danced for me and bear-hugged me, sending away any worries I had about spending my birthday alone in another country. That moment made me realize that it didn't take much to make me happy. It was all about the simple things.

Two weeks later, April's pain from dengue returned, a vicious virus she caught from a mosquito. She developed a fever and experienced pain in her muscles and joints. She couldn't function on her own and was barely able to move. So I packed a bag for a week and served her the best way I knew how.

I planned her meals each day, which taught me to pay attention to details and stay within a grocery budget. Serving April gave me a love for cooking, which became my outlet for self-care.

A few weeks later, Tasha and her mom visited me for a few days. Tasha coming to visit me meant the world to me because she got to see what letting me drive her SUV to that small group produced for my first trip to the Dominican Republic.

A month and a half later, Momma and my sister Ashley visited, leaving Summer at home because she had to work. This trip was good for Momma because she'd never flown on an airplane or been outside the United States. I was happy to see Momma smile, much like she did at

Christmas time when we were younger. It was a glimpse into the life I'd one day give her.

When they arrived, I gave them a tour of my life in the Dominican Republic. They needed to experience what I experienced to see that I was safe, loved, and cared for by the people there.

I let them try the La Bandera, the Dominican dish I learned how to cook when I first got there. We walked the streets and rode in all three forms of transportation. They even met the little girls who changed my life.

Momma didn't say too much about what she thought about my life there. She didn't have to say much because her immediate silence showed me that she was taking it all in.

Traveling wasn't new to Ashley. She smiled at what she saw, but she had questions about the food and my safety.

All in all, I knew they were happy to be with me again, and I was delighted to be with them again.

Momma and Ashley booked a room at a resort for the week, so after showing them my life there, we returned to my apartment to get my bag so that I could stay with them. We saw the little girls waiting for me when we approached my door. We all walked into my apartment, but they went crazy when they saw me get my bag.

Dory and Ada blocked my doorway so that I couldn't get out. Rose and Brandy searched my apartment for my passport to ensure I wasn't leaving the Dominican Republic, and Lisa was arguing in Spanish with Momma. For a moment, things calmed down, but then, out of nowhere, when I opened my front door, they all rushed me, pulling my bag off my back and trying to hold me hostage.

Ashley sat there, hysterical and recording it all.

After fifteen minutes of calming them down and explaining to them I'd only be gone for a few days, for the first time in my life I questioned if I wanted to have kids. Because although they showed me love and I knew how to love them, caring for children comes with great responsibility.

A few days after Momma and Ashley left to go back home, the reality that I was leaving soon to go back home too got real.

Had I done enough?
Did I learn everything I was supposed to learn?
Was I ready to go back home?

These questions flooded my mind, and the answer to every one of them was no. I had a burning desire to stay a bit longer, and I also had no plan career-wise when I got back home.

I had options, but I wanted to stay in the Dominican Republic.

I did what I knew how: prayed for my next steps.

I went on a ten-day fast. I turned off my phone and held onto what God showed me, which didn't make sense. He showed me that I'd be living in a different country again, and I thought it was lining up for me to stay in the Dominican Republic.

During my first five months in the Dominican Republic, I slept on an air mattress. Surprisingly on the last day of my fast, a missionary gave me a bed frame and a mattress. That night I thanked God for a bed and finally got to rest.

I went to work the following day, sure of what God showed me. I approached my boss and told him what I was feeling.

"I *feel* like I'm supposed to continue working with you all here in the Dominican Republic," I told him.

"Amber, it's funny that you tell me this because there is a meeting about hiring you as an administrative assistant," he said, smiling and affirming what I knew God had shown me.

This meeting confirmed the word I knew God was giving me.

I was moving to the Dominican Republic.

I didn't let that news remain a secret for long. After telling my family and friends I was moving, I created a plan by putting my faith into action and preparing for my permanent move to the Dominican Republic.

I had a designer create a fundraising document, I sent emails, and I planned to go back home for two months to say my goodbyes to everyone. In the wake of such good news, I felt the pressure to say goodbye to the life I built in the Dominican Republic for a while.

A few weeks later, I stepped out onto my balcony, where it all began, and I allowed myself to feel all the emotions that came with that day.

How did a girl like me get here? I kept asking myself again.

Six years prior, I wanted to end my life, and now I was walking in my purpose, experiencing life and its fullness. I couldn't do anything but cry.

As I stepped back inside my apartment, I noticed the little foot marks on my kitchen floor had disappeared. Locals picked up my furniture that I had sold or given away, and my bags were packed and waiting for me at the door. I was now standing in an empty apartment, emptied of everything I came with and everything I once thought I needed.

I headed back to the United States.

———

April's gray Suzuki pulled up to my apartment to take me to the airport. As I gathered my bags, I heard Rose screaming for me to come outside.

"Amber no puedes ir por que tengo algo para ti," she insisted, begging me to come to her house for a gift she had for me.

When I got to the front door, she grabbed my arms and told me to stand there and wait for her. She walked backward toward one of the walls in their home and grabbed one of her mom's decorative butterflies off the wall. She walked back to me, holding a red, black, and white glittery butterfly.

"Esto es para ti. Dios sabe," telling me the butterfly was for me and God knew. She wiped the tears from her eyes and attempted to wipe the tears falling from mine. I thanked her, crying like I wasn't coming back.

I stood there, holding the butterfly in my hands, reminiscing. I became that little girl in the backyard again, watching my caterpillar come out from its cocoon and become a butterfly.

Even though I knew I was returning to the Dominican Republic in two months, I was emotional. Saying goodbye to who I wasn't anymore made me emotional, but it was beautiful. I wasn't, and I'll never be the same.

I continued to cry as April drove away. I was no longer the caterpillar who desperately needed to crawl into the cocoon. I was leaving Tierra Dominicana aware of how far I'd come and conscious of where I was going.

12

Returning

It was close to midnight on a Monday in the summer of 2017 when I got back home. I came back home fifteen pounds heavier, liberated, and healthy. A three-thousand dollar check from Mrs. Kimberly and her husband awaited me for my relocation to the Dominican Republic. The money was more confirmation that the journey I was on was correct.

I was on another mission, and this time, it was to say goodbye to my family and friends and raise the money I needed for my move back. However, when I got up the following morning, nothing about home felt like home.

As I walked down the stairs to my car, I had a weird flashback of the car accident in high school. My heart raced as I tried to figure out what that flashback meant. I was a dreamer, and God spoke to me through dreams, so I was troubled when I had a flashback instead. My back stiffened, and my head hurt. Something wasn't right.

The next day, I tried not to let fear creep in, as I was still feeling the weight of this flashback. So I prayed, went on my morning run, then ordered my usual chicken biscuit from Chick-fil-A. I picked up some hair extensions and headed to Elosie's shop to get my hair done. I was getting my hair done to stop me from manipulating my hair while I was home.

As I got near the Chevron on Highway 119, I got a strong urge to pray, so I did.

I barely made it past the Chevron when a car coming out of the gas station struck the right side of my car. My car hydroplaned, and my mind spun with it. I tried controlling the wheel -- something I now know not to do -- and realized my car was headed straight for oncoming traffic. I didn't see an end to this accident, so at twenty-four years old, I prayed one of the boldest prayers I'd ever prayed: *God, if this is how my life ends, please let me go out without feeling anything.*

My spirit jumped, and I heard the words, "Let go."

I let go of the wheel.

My car did one final spin, stopping me on the other side of the road, in the opposite direction than what I was traveling. My car made a side-by-side impact with a guard rail.

I walked away with a sprained wrist and a totaled car. The accident had set the tone for my return home. This return was something for which I didn't prepare.

RETURNING

I spent the next few weeks trying to express how I changed and what I learned during those six months in the Dominican Republic, but no one would truly understand. It was hard to explain what someone had to experience for themselves, and I didn't want to be misunderstood by those who'd never gone. So on most days, I sat in silence without anyone to understand my experiences.

Momma and my sisters thought I had an attitude, which strained our relationships most of the time. We fought without words as they tried to understand why I struggled in a place that should've felt like home. My experiences of growth and transformation in the Dominican Republic holistically positively affected me, and nothing at home was the same. Nothing would ever be the same, and I didn't know how to explain that to them.

I was furious with them because I wanted them to understand why I stayed quiet. I also couldn't expect someone to understand the transformation inside of me. My growth was for me, not them. Besides, I had to understand that I wasn't the only one growing and transforming; their growth and transformation just looked different from mine.

Now back at square one - and understanding I'd never have it all figured out and I'd always grow - I learned the importance of giving myself grace. As I grieved my way through, trying to make sense of what was happening, Jamese reminded me that *this* - everlearning - was the true summit of life.

After my car was totaled, I was left carless, and Jamese let me use her car to finish what I came back home to do.

One evening, she came over and sat with me.

"Amber, you being back home has significance, and no matter how you want to look at it, *home* is still and will always be a priority," Jamese said. "If you can't nurture your relationships with your family, you have no business going back to the other side of the world to be in a relationship with others."

That truth hurt. I didn't want to believe it, but I knew she was right.

———

ONE EVENING, WHILE WAITING for Jamese to get off work, Mrs. Kimberly asked me to share my testimony with a group of high school students at her church the following week. Nervous but sure that I had to do it, I said yes and made that drive to Gordo, Alabama, a few days later.

As I went to the stage to speak, I didn't stand on the stage. I put the chair on the floor and sat in it. I wondered what a woman like me was doing seated behind a microphone.

I sat in that black chair behind that microphone, with my stomach turning in knots and my heels tapping on the rails of the chair. I don't know why I didn't ask for bottled water before sitting down, but I needed one. I had cottonmouth, and all I wanted was something to quench my thirst. I was more nervous than I should've been.

When I heard gum pop from the back of the room, it reminded me of being a little girl on that stage sharing

RETURNING

my story in the third grade, when everyone waited for me to speak.

It was time for me to speak.

Once again, much like that time Mr. D. told me to share my testimony in the Dominican Republic, I put aside the message I practiced and said what I needed to say, for the students.

Those students heard my testimony in its entirety. I told them how my upbringing defined me so long that I couldn't be my most authentic self. I told them how not understanding love led me to look for love in all the wrong places. I told them that college was less about my degree and more about who I'd become. I shared how not knowing myself prevented me from embracing my purpose.

They had no idea I was scared as I shared the most vulnerable pieces of me. Or maybe they did. Regardless, they needed to hear the testimony of someone close to their age overcoming obstacles and hardship, so I did it scared.

When I finished, the leaders told the students to speak with me if they needed to. I found myself sitting alone on a two-seat couch in the back of the room.

As the minutes went by, the number of students in the room decreased. I figured the students didn't need to talk to me, so I gathered my things and got ready to leave. As I picked up my purse and headed for the door, God told me to sit down because it wasn't time for me to go yet.

I had no idea who, what, or why I was waiting, but I waited five more minutes. As I bit my nails, anxiously waiting, I saw a young lady walking toward me. My heart went out to her because she didn't have to say anything before sitting next to me - I could see the hurt and pain in her eyes. I could see it because I could see myself at her age.

"Hey, you can sit here," I said as I put my purse and journal on the floor.

After a few minutes of silence between us, she began to speak.

"The things you shared with us made me feel like I wasn't alone," she said, holding her head down.

She wasn't alone.

She was a student a few years younger than me, and my being there was for her. She was desperate for someone to listen to her and give her hope through the same life experiences I had - lack of identity, hurt, betrayal, and fear. She needed to hear my story of how I was still trying to embrace my God-given identity so I could fulfill my purpose. We had way more in common than either of us thought, and we were thankful to be in the same space of acceptance.

That conversation between us two brought me to complete silence on my drive back home. My tears stained my blue-and-white-striped peplum top, conviction softly hugged me, and God did what He always does: He spoke.

He showed me that a plague of fear almost prevented me from sharing the depths of who I was. I'd prayed to be authentic, but I wasn't yet ready. Authenticity brings with it a higher responsibility. I had to get vulnerable for someone else's healing, making my story no longer about me.

For a second, my logic seemed bizarre until I remembered the day I almost ended my life. Suddenly,

RETURNING

what appeared irrational became necessary. It's not about being heard over the microphone, but instead having the eyes and ears to see and hear that *one*.

As I reflected over my journey in the car that day, I concluded that someone had always reached back and picked me up when I was at my lowest. And it was time for me to go back and empower someone else to come out on the other side as I did.

A few weeks later, I made myself an office at one of the local coffee shops. I had a conference call that day with one of the leaders I'd be working for when I returned to the Dominican Republic. I couldn't wait for this day because it reminded me that I had less than a month left in Alabama.

I was ready to go.

My phone started vibrating the table, and I got excited. I picked it up and answered the phone.

"Hello," I said, anticipating what the conversation held.

"Amber, it's so good to hear from you," he said, thanking me for my work in the Dominican Republic already.

"No, thank you," I replied. I was more thankful for the opportunity to serve them. After telling him about my fundraising success, he commended me for saying yes to this part of my life. What he said next, though, immediately caused my stomach to hurt. I was sick.

"I see the skills you possess and how you can add to the organization, and we're so excited to have you," he said, clearly excited for my return. "We are looking forward to your return, but you must know that after budget reviews, we can't pay you for a year. We can revisit the salary for your role once you've reached your year mark."

I had no words. I was in disbelief, trying to process what I'd just heard. Immediately I had to use the bathroom.

None of this aligned with what God had shown me while in the Dominican Republic. I sat there searching for a response to his words, but my mind was racing at 90 mph, and I couldn't think of anything to say.

Disbelief zipped my mouth tight, but I had so many questions.

I was angry because I left my entire life in April's house, on the other side of the world, and I didn't have a plan for this side. That wasn't rejection. It was the murky middle ground, and I had no idea where I was going.

I mustered up the words to respond, even though they were few.

"Thank you for letting me know about the change," I replied, telling him that I'd get back with him by the end of the week on what I decided to do.

I hung up the phone, buried my face into the corner of the booth, and I cried.

I felt like I'd been slapped in the face again. I said yes and meant it.

I had questions, but perhaps all God wanted was my yes.

When I sought God for my next steps months before, He showed me I'd relocate to another country, but it wasn't in the timing or where I thought. So as I worked my way through this disappointment, I decided to leave my next steps, whatever they were, in God's hands.

I prepared for this moment, and I knew what I needed to do. It wasn't what I wanted to do because I knew that coming home would take more out of me than working on the other side of the world.

I'D BEEN BACK HOME FOR A FEW MONTHS. I said goodbyes to the life I built in the Dominican Republic, and I forgot about the butterfly Rose gave me.

Most of my days were difficult because I had no idea what was next. The same degree I paid for was the same degree that left me jobless for months. I applied for jobs I was overqualified for but didn't get. So I found myself flipping burgers and cleaning out fryers at Whataburger.

I was trying to understand where I was and why, so I pushed my love for writing aside. When I wasn't working overnight at Whataburger, I stayed in hotels to get away. I needed to be alone because I knew no one understood me. They couldn't.

I could count on one hand how many times I went to church. The church had become routine to me, rather than actual worship to God, and I was too mad at God.

I kissed social media goodbye for six months because my identity and worth went beyond social media. What was going on in my heart was more important than what people saw. I stopped engaging in virtual reality and engaged in my reality. Being back home under these circumstances was interesting, and it became more interesting when I got up one morning for a workday at the coffee shop.

I made my way down the stairs to the car, but I didn't have my keys. I stood at the driver-side door, searching my jacket pockets. I shook my bag and realized they were on the ground. When I bent down to pick them up, I noticed my keys weren't keys but a yellow-and-black snake. The snake wrapped its body around my hand, and before it could bite me, I threw it off.

I sat on the edge of my bed, in a frenzy, and I realized I was dreaming.

Of all my dreams, this one shook me the most.

When the sun came up, I sought wise counsel from my mentor about what this dream could mean.

She told me my car keys represented new opportunities waiting for me. They represented me going somewhere fast. The parked car had power, but the car could use the power if I used the keys to start it. My purpose was the car, and the only way I'd get to the new opportunities was to turn the car on, activating my purpose.

The keys were on the ground because I let go of God's plan for me somewhere in my journey back home. After all, life wasn't going according to *my* plan.

The keys became a yellow and black snake, representing error and wisdom. The keys-turned-snake also meant the heaviness that came with pursuing my purpose. I had a powerful gift of faith and discernment, but it'd be up to my surrender to activate it. I had to trust God's plan to bring me back home.

RETURNING

    This dream had nothing but the truth. My lack of understanding of why I was back home, when I thought I was moving to the Dominican Republic, stopped me from picking up the keys to my purpose. I was so distracted by my altered plans; I forgot I still had work to do back at home. I had a purpose, even if it looked different than I thought. I owned my car, my ambition, but I couldn't start it because I didn't know which way to go. So I created other plans, which took me on a different route than God's plan for me. That was the error.

    I felt stuck and complacent even when I did what should've made me feel purposeful. I sought to be corrected almost to an unhealthy point, and I apologized so much I no longer knew what I was apologizing for. Sometimes my desire to do everything right prevented me from doing anything at all. It wasn't the fear of failing others that caused me to stop; it was the fear of failing myself and God, even after doing all the work to get here.

    That revelation gave me the truth I needed the most – *I hadn't arrived; I'd only just begun.*

13

Beginning

Let's take a seat and get some coffee. If you don't like coffee, grab a cup of tea, water, a smoothie, or whatever you like because I want you to be comfortable. No, I need you to be comfortable.

Are you comfortable? Okay, good.

Now, let's talk.

As you go through life, pull up a chair and break bread with yourself first before feeding someone else. Whether we want to admit it, we can't grow if we don't give ourselves space to heal. Our shortcomings and insecurities will always be on us to address, and if we don't deal with them, they'll always be what holds us back from reaching our potential.

HUPOMONE

Be as committed to your process as you are to what the process will produce in you and for you. Choose not to give up on what you're enduring and know that what you're going through is connected to someone you're supposed to pull through.

Every rejection brings with it a gift. Look for that gift. That gift is there, you just have to find it.

Make space for the unknown to fill up places in your life.

Take note of your training, your upbringing, and make a conscious decision to let go of what doesn't make you better. Assess what you need to let go of in your life and write it down. Ultimately, what influences your life becomes your life.

When temptation knocks at your door, have a plan to defeat it. Be mindful of its nature, and try your hardest not to bite its bait. Temptation has learned from your past mistakes; it doesn't like you and seeks to control you. Know the person you'll call to help you when tempted.

Connect with people beyond what you see on the surface. Say hi to them, learn their names, their story. Every individual you meet has a story. Sit down and open their book. If you don't like what you read on the first page, don't close the book. Instead, turn the page.

The world we live in has a way of turning the best of us into people we never thought we'd be. When you understand that, you'll realize that most people deemed evil didn't become evil by choice. They are human, just like you. They were just beaten down by what hurt them.

BEGINNING

It's equally important to note that sometimes people won't connect with you, and that's okay. Don't allow the opinions of others to make you forget who you are. Look at yourself in the mirror and remind yourself of who God made you to be. Those people don't know you; they believe who you were is who you'll always be. Be free from the opinions of others because those who don't understand the grace of God will never know how you can fall and still get back up.

The friends you do life with are essential. You'll become a byproduct of those relationships - make sure they are good for you.

It's normal and healthy to want to grow, and it's unhealthy to be in the same place you were five years ago. You'll lose friends as you continue to grow, people you never thought you'd lose. Sometimes, the ones who helped you get there won't always be there to win with you. Be gracious to them. No matter how things ended, you wouldn't be who you are today without them.

Shame and condemnation are not of God; conviction is. And if you don't recognize that and test its fruit, it'll have you trading God's truth about who you are for the enemy's lies and who he wants you to be. Stand firm.

Stop feeling guilty about the questions you want God to answer. Ask them and be okay with not getting the answers immediately. God cares about your pain and your questions.

Love can be scary when hurt from it is all you know. Trauma in love teaches you that if it's not hard all the time, then it's not right. That is false. Love will be challenging, but with God, love can be beautiful. If the love you saw growing up has scarred you, heal from that trauma so that you don't cause wounds to others. Identify what happened to you and how it wounded you. Assess the coping mechanisms you took on to protect yourself. Be honest with yourself and heal from that trauma. Heal from that trauma so you can experience love in its most beautiful form.

Love will reveal to you your most shadow self. Don't run from it. Don't hide when you see who you are because it's trying to teach you something. If you allow it, love will grow you and expand you.

Seek to uncover the hidden parts of said person in love, in your relationships. Some things were there before you encountered them. It's important not to miss the step of seeing them and discovering them, first. Ask the hard questions and be okay if the answers make you uncomfortable. To some, that can be scary; that's okay. Growing and becoming in love takes time. Stay gentle with yourself. God's got you!

You aren't too much for love. You deserve love. You deserve to be with someone willing to see the ugliest parts of you and still choose to love you. Don't push them away when they still choose to love you. Love shows you differences, and those differences in walks of life don't make you or that person wrong. It just makes you different, and that's okay.

Seeking to be right in love will always get in the way of the kind of peace an apology can do for love. Listen before

BEGINNING

you speak, even if you are right. Choose communication in love, even when it's hard so that you can connect with that person.

Love doesn't make you compromise who you are. It seeks to preserve who you are while bringing out the best in you. Love doesn't ask you to be perfect; it asks you to be willing to grow. Two imperfect individuals, willing to work together to become more excellent versions of themselves daily, can change the world.

Love doesn't pull you away from your purpose but instead pushes you into it. Love is safe, and if you don't feel safe there, don't settle there.

Think about what you want in love, and discern if the love presented is what you want. If it's not, you have to be okay with walking away. If it is, you have to allow yourself to give love and receive love. Love is a choice, and when you give yourself to love, it will cost you some things, some growth. Just make sure that it doesn't cost you your identity.

Allow love to honor you, cover you, and protect you. Allow love to be easy because God is love and His love is easy.

Self-awareness and the willingness to grow is key.

Don't aim to be bigger; strive to be better every day.

Take a road trip, take a day off work, or take a walk in the park.

Be still and allow yourself to learn. Absorb wisdom from those that came before you; their wisdom are proverbs and jewels that can help you for your journey ahead.

HUPOMONE

Life is fleeting, and we'll all leave this place someday, so be in God's will for your life and enjoy the ride along the way. When it's all said and done, all you'll have is your experiences.

Stay inspired.
Be bold.
Be radical.
Take risks.
Open yourself up to what's on the other side of the leap.

Your highest calling is becoming who God has designed you to be, and serving others while you do it. Surrender what you think will happen and let your life play out how it's supposed to because it will.

Allow yourself to run through the rain because you just might learn everything you need for the person you're becoming.

―

There once was a time when I lived in the shadows of how people viewed me. I often shrunk in my strength as a black woman because they said it was too strong. My "resting face" made people believe something was wrong with me, and frequently there was. I was hurt because I lost a sense of myself in facing myself. I've hurt people in the same way they've hurt me, but I dare not shame those places because those places made me who I am today.

BEGINNING

I understand I didn't get where I am today alone. The love from my people not giving up on me has helped me stay the course. God brought me this far, and He didn't leave me. His unfailing love in the pursuit of my heart, even when I was resistant, let me know He'd always be with me.

I understand that I can't be found in love until it sees me there first. When love sees me, I don't run from it. I discover it and let it unravel. I'm learning to be patient with myself in the process.

I believe in the power of healing and what healing can do in the deepest places of our souls. I yearn for meaningful conversations, wisdom, and knowledge for the days ahead because I know that there is someone who can always teach me something.

Misunderstanding happens, but a fierceness lives deep in my soul that is irrevocable. I'm bold and unashamed of everything that has led me here today. I'm not in a rush for what society says I should have or be by now. I understand, now, that everything has its set time and season, and I choose to rest in that, even when it's hard. God revealed that I'll always be His girl, and I don't have to figure it all out because He already has; I just have to be obedient and trust Him. It is all *still* a process.

I've got some scars but I'm called, and I rise imperfectly every day to the occasion. For I understand that when I reach a level of comfort, I'll come undone again, pick up the pieces, and keep growing.

~

I am created in the image of the Most High God, for He lives inside of me.

I am a woman on a mission.

As I surrendered to my faith in God and His plans for my life, I was able to embrace my identity and fulfill my purpose. I no longer wait for the rain to pass; instead, I sit with myself first, and then run through *it* because I know when I endure, I'll get to where I'm supposed to be. *That is Hupomone.*

I haven't become, for I'm just beginning, and it all had to be this way.

So, tell me, who are you? What is your story?

AFTERWORD

A Thank You from Amber

When God first told me I'd write a book, I laughed. While I had a passion for words, I didn't set my mind on using my words to inspire people. I knew the standard of the book He called me to write -- vulnerable and authentic -- and I didn't want to be the one to write it. I didn't want to be vulnerable before others in a setting where pain once resided. I can't blame the old me, though, because I'd learned to mask the truth with a smile and seal the deal in prayer.

Writing this book has been one of the hardest things to date. I spent five years feeling it all, healing from it all, and learning to believe in myself again.

I spent some days writing on my futon in the Dominican Republic, drenched in sweat because of my concrete home. Other days were spent in my bed in Mexico, on my second trip there in 2019. My butt was numb, and my legs were limp and throbbing because I was physically tired of walking in the heat all day. At the end of writing this book, I spent my days editing in my room at Momma's house, in parking lots with a WiFi connection, hotels, or a friend's home, finally realizing I must be my most authentic self when I write. In the midst of all this, I lost the manuscript several times and consequently penned what God gave me. I was writing, erasing, and writing some more.

My chapters frequently turned into ugly cries before I could write more. They forced me to relive experiences to forgive myself for the hurt I caused myself and others. Sometimes, I couldn't define what I was experiencing, and being honest with you, I thought I was depressed throughout the writing process. But I've learned not to mistake depression for healing that comes in a different form. I discovered there was healing beyond me because God restoring me wasn't just for me. He showed me you, the deep-down you that you don't even realize deserves redemption.

The manuscript I previously wrote was accepted, only to go through a series of rejections. What I wrote had good intentions, but I wasn't writing at the God-called level. I had to release myself from the style of writing I thought was expected of me: *fancy and not me*. Those rejections weren't a reflection of who I am but instead challenged me to tap into who and whose I am.

I immersed myself in learning what I could about the writing industry. I studied authors, my mistakes, and sought to improve where I failed. I attended conferences, enrolled in a writing program, and read articles and books by rejected authors. I let my editor in on my life, and she

BEGINNING

helped me write like me. I realized I wasn't the author they were looking for, and I had a choice to make: I could sit and drown myself in the rejections pool or get up and do the work. These things unleashed me into a much more profound revelation of myself. The process of rewriting this book was exhilarating.

Although fragments of who I once was will always remind me of what I did and what happened to me, the redeeming power of Jesus Christ, and my tribe, will always be what saved me. If my greatest work on this side of life is inspiring you through this book, then I've completed the work and I hope it inspires you.

Thank you, for it was you that pushed me to my completion.

We did this.

ACKNOWLEDGMENTS

As I've previously stated, writing this book has been one of *the* hardest things I've set my heart, mind, body, and soul to do. I know that it wouldn't be in your hands if it weren't for the many people who stood by me.

Abba Father, thank you for pursuing me when I was resistant to your leading. Thank you for always helping me find my way back to you. As stated throughout this book, I know my journey; this book is because you spoke to me because you love me, you had a purpose beyond me, and I chose to yield to your will for my life. I owe you everything I have, everything I am, and everything I will become. Thank you for saving me.

Momma, growing up, I couldn't understand why you raised us the way you did, but I'm so thankful for it all today. I know I didn't help the burdens you had to carry at times but thank you for withstanding them with such grit and grace. Thank you for teaching me how to make something out of nothing. Without you, I wouldn't be the woman I am today. I'm going to give you the world.

Daddy, as a baby, you carried me, and as a little girl, you sang with me. Today, your morning phone calls still make me smile. Because of you, I know perseverance. Thank you for giving me the space to embrace who I've always been. I'll forever be your little girl. This book is a product of what you produced.

Big Daddy, while losing you broke my heart, I won't wait to live another moment because I know you wouldn't want me waiting. I'll continue singing and dancing it out when the storms of life rage against me because I know God is with me. This book is for you.

Porcia, we were in the second grade when you asked my mom if I peed in the bed at night because one day I came to school smelling like pee. I never told you, but I did pee in the bed. I laugh at it now because your heart for the truth helped set me free. Losing you at such a young age hurt, and not understanding your death almost led me to my own. I write these words on the other side, thanking you for such a rare and honest friendship. This book is because of you.

Grandma Dorethia and Uncle Thomas, the way you both have sown into my life go beyond words. If it weren't for your love, prayers, wisdom first, and constant helping hands second, I honestly don't know where I'd be. Thank you for teaching me what it means to show up and believe that good things happen.

To my Sisters and Brother, Gabrielle, Nyeshia, Autumn, Maua, and Gavin, thank you for loving me and all my ways. Each of our relationships is unique, and that uniqueness makes me so proud to be your sister. Thank you for teaching me what protection from a sibling looked like at an early age. Thank you for keeping all my secrets and telling on me when you were mad at me. Thank you for understanding my need to go and always supporting me along the way. I pray that I've made you proud because you have made me proud. Our best days are ahead of us.

My Pastor and First Lady, Rodney and Connie Brown, the night I tried suicide, you drove down to

BEGINNING

Tuscaloosa and sat in that cold room with me in the middle of the night. You didn't say much, and you didn't have to because your presence was everything I needed. Since I was a little girl, being under you has molded me into the woman of faith I am today. I know leading a flock comes with great responsibility, but I pray that this book is a reminder that the call you all answered will always be worth it. Thank you for praying for me and speaking over my life.

Mrs. Kimberly Sanders, my freshman year of college, you saw something in me that I didn't see in myself, and you took me in as your own. When I had no fight left in me, you told me to go before God and yield to Him. Surrendering to Him has made me who I am today. You and Mr. Roddy supported every international trip I took, you both opened up your home to me, you both made sure I remained steadfast in God's will, and you both are why this book has happened. Thank you, just thank you. Everything I set my hands to, I owe you.

Uncle Nefer and Aunt Elvie, when I had no idea how I'd return to school my freshman year of college, you both willingly invested in my education. You were some of the first examples I had, and you made sure I understood the importance of paying back what I owed. Today you've invested in my love for all things culture, the arts, and holistic healing. Thank you for being a safe space for me to be open. Thank you for seeing me and who I'd become before I got there.

My Very Best Friends, My Tribe, and My Persons, I don't deserve any of you but my heart dances because you all believe I do. Thank you for putting up with me not answering the phone and understanding my need to be alone, still. Thank you for understanding my need to be obedient to God, to go where He leads me. Thank you for forcing me to sit down and face myself. Thank you for giving me the shoulders to cry on when I'm sad and the space to dance it out when I'm happy. Thank you for letting me crash at your places to write and finish this book. Thank you for not leaving me when I so deserved it. Thank you for loving me, even when I didn't know how to love myself. Thank you for believing in this book, even when I didn't. We're only going up from here, together – "lets goooooo!"

To the People who invested in my mission work, business, and journey, thank you for trusting that what you sowed was being sown on good ground. Thank you for helping birth Hupomone. What you blessed me with, you will see a tenfold blessing. Watch it manifest.

Jill McCormick, I don't even know if there'd be a physical book without you. The months of editing you walked through with me wasn't just editing. It was heart surgery, it was understanding the depths of who I am, and I was getting the story right within myself first before I put it on paper. It was nights of consistently reworking completed manuscripts because the drive crashed. Every email, every voice message, and prayer will always mean more to me than you'll ever know. Thank you for empowering me to go from Fiction to Nonfiction. I'm so glad you prayed before you began working with me because I know that if it weren't for your prayers, I wouldn't be the author I am today. You are Heaven Sent!

BEGINNING

Taylor Grater, every time you took a picture of me, you helped me see the growth that was taking place inside of me, showing up on the outside of me. Thank you for catching me on the front cover, in my most honest form. You have a gift and are a true gem.

Mollie Blackwood, thank you for not only designing this book cover but also teaching me a thing or two about sensitivity to one's artwork. Your hands and your heart for art are rare and needed. Thank you for capturing me, the whole me, and bringing it to life with this book design.

Jasmine Prince, thank you for believing in this project when it looked like it wasn't going to happen. Your gift of creating space for others and bringing ideas and visions to life, through design, helped shape this project; thank you for handling my project with care. Thank you for creating a safe space for me to *ditch fear and embrace the risk* so that I could grow as a woman and creative. Thank you for holding me accountable and reminding me that this book has to come out. Thank you for partnering with me from beginning to end. Here's to our friendship, growth, and the purpose work ahead of us!

Kayla Hamlett, you came into my life at a time where I was lifeless. I was just coming up for air when you threw the life vest that pulled me back into my purpose. You were my second chance at getting mentorship and leadership right and I'm honored that you trusted me with your heart, your soul, and your spirit. Having a front row seat to the woman that you've become is a true blessing and I don't take your love for granted. Thank you for being the mastermind of all things press for this project; your skillset is why we are going where we are going. Your prayers, accountability, encouragement, and leadership are why this project has become what it is. Here's to the glory ahead.

Timothy and the T&J Publishing Team, thank you for working with me, being patient with me, and having an eye for detail. Your promise to "turn publishing dreams into reality" has manifested and I couldn't have asked for a better company to publish my debut book. In fact, I don't believe anyone else could've done it like you all. Thank you!

Cameron, my first love, your presence was heavy in the final stages of producing this book. You occasionally sat in parking lots with me to get it done, and you gave me constructive criticism on the parts that could be better, even when it was hard for me to see it like that. You opened my eyes to what it means to love, even when my trauma in love tried to prevent me from experiencing it. The same love I was afraid of you showed me could one day be safe when two people are self-aware and willing to grow. Thank you for opening my heart to seeing me so that I could give the best of myself in love. Thank you for loving me. I will always love you!

To my Unborn Children, my Niece Serenity Grace, my God-son Grayson Eugene, and all my Girls in the Dominican Republic, when you become of age to understand what I've written in this book, may these words empower you to never settle for less than what you deserve. I love each of you with everything in me and I can't wait to see who you all become. This book is for you all!

To the Early Bird Readers of Hupomone, thank you for taking on the task of diving into my book before

BEGINNING

the world did. Your eyes helped me see errors that my eyes missed. Your willingness taught me more of what it means to believe in someone and show up for them. Without you all reading my book, the world wouldn't have it in its most pure form. You are all the real MVPs!

The People I met at the University of Alabama are so many to name, but you know who you are. It's because of the love that you showed me that I was able to stand firm during my time there. May the memories never fade, and the love always remains. Thank you for some of the greatest moments of my life!

To my Teachers and Mentors, your mentorship and selfless love made it easy for me to listen to those who have gone before me. Life wouldn't be the same without your never-ending wisdom, hugs when we passed, the likes and comments on social media, and random check-ins. Thank you for teaching me how to be a student in life.

Thank you to the People I once had the Opportunity to Walk Alongside. No matter how things shifted and ended in our relationships, your relationship and what you taught me was good for my becoming, and I hope it was good for yours. You'll always have a special place in my heart.

To Every Person that Will Read This Book, my ultimate prayer is that my story inspires and empowers you to go after God and who He has called you to be. May you dismantle the hurt that has been standing in the way of your becoming. You can become now.

To the Hupomone Collective, no matter how bad the storm gets, may we always run through it to get to our destinies.

ABOUT THE AUTHOR

Born in Birmingham and raised in Alabaster, Alabama, Amber Underwood is a trailblazer, empowering women to embrace their God-given identity so they can fulfill the purpose for their life. She is a woman on a mission, businesswoman, writer, and social servant involved in various sectors of the community. She vulnerably shares her journey of yielding to faith for the sake of her becoming because she desires for people to become the most phenomenal versions of themselves.

Amber is a two-time graduate of the University of Alabama at Tuscaloosa, where her journey of higher learning became the voyage to awaken her purpose. She is an avid coffee drinker who enjoys reading books, dancing, camping out in coffee shops, growing through life's lessons, and traveling globally. No matter where life takes her, she will always reach back for one, hoping to empower somebody as someone empowered her. *For she knows that if you allow yourself to go through it, you might learn everything you need for the person you're becoming.*

www.ingramcontent.com/pod-product-compliance
Lightning Source LLC
Chambersburg PA
CBHW031242290426
44109CB00012B/402